THE O...
HIGH-...
HANDBOOK

(How to Succeed in Business *without* an MBA)

by

Philip Jenks

Jim Fisk

Robert Barron

Cartoons by Jonathan Pugh

A HARRIMAN HOUSE BOOK

HARRIMAN HOUSE PUBLISHING 071 371 7598

'THE OFFICIAL HIGH-FLIER'S HANDBOOK' by Philip Jenks, Jim Fisk and Robert Barron : Copyright Harriman House Publishing 1993.

Thanks to :
• Graham Jones of The Company Writers for his observations on annual reports and accounts
• Patricia Morison and the Financial Times for help with the section on management survival courses
• Chris Beresford and KPMG for help with the section on Accounting

---

British Library Cataloguing-in-Publication Data

A CIP record for this book is available from the British Library.

ISBN 1-897597-01-0

Printed and bound in Great Britain by

Holbrook & Son
Norway Rd
Hilsea
Portsmouth
Hants
PO3 5HX

CONTENTS

Part Five
CAREER MANAGEMENT

Part Six
KEEPING SCORE

Part Seven
BUZZWORD GLOSSARY

INTRODUCTION

THE DESIRE TO GET AHEAD in business is stimulated at an early age. Remember that intoxicating moment when you first managed to nab Mayfair and Park Lane, get a hotel on each, and send your opponent headlong into bankruptcy as he landed on one after the other? Remember the sheer thrill of it when you bartered two Sherbert Fountains for a champion conker and ten minutes later leveraged it for a 16-function Victorinox penknife? It's a fact that the very best childhood memories tend to be materialistic, competitive and exploitative in nature — in short, capitalist.

Recapturing those thrills is more elusive in the *real* game of business. It's a tough world out there, the rules are strictly enforced, and the competition's a little sharper than when you skittled Granny out of the game with some shrewd double-sixes. If you want to be a high-flier in today's business world, you've

got to have a good grasp of the fundamentals — like how to *talk* and how to *look* — and at least have a nodding aquaintance with peripheral matters like finance and marketing. Otherwise, in no time at all, you'll find yourself surrounded by colleagues babbling in tongues you don't understand and leapfrogging you on their way to the top.

The publishing industry knows a gravy train when it sees one, and in the past decade, great forests of redwoods have been sacrificed on the altar of business education. The most successful self-help books never go out of print, and are studied like sacramental texts by successive generations of ambitious managers. So many millions of copies have been sold that it's hard to imagine how people like Richard Branson and Anita Roddick managed to scrape together their multi-million pound fortunes without knowing whether their complexions suited Winter or

Summer colours.

The business book explosion isn't necessarily a bad thing, but you have to ask whether all the theoretical knowledge being ingested is actually making any difference to management effectiveness. We may be more boned up than the Italians on T.Q.M., but they still make very nice sweaters; no-one's ever had much to say for French negotiation techniques, but at least they've got an indigenous motor industry; Greek speed-reading courses are still in their infancy, but they build some of the world's biggest oil-tankers.

The UK, meanwhile, for all its erudition, drifts ever lower down the world GDP league.

Given our indifferent economic performance, there's at least an arguable case that all these business books do is stodge up creative thinking and waste management time. And when you consider that most of their authors never enjoyed real business success themselves until their books hit the big time, you have to wonder just why everyone pays so much attention to them.

This book is aimed at business executives everywhere who are feeling confused, constipated and ripped off by existing business literature. Our aim is revisionist and puritanical : to purge business publishing of its excess verbiage, to sort the nuggets from the sludge, to tell you what you need to know, and discard the rest.

Quite a lot has been discarded : just as it takes 250 tons of ore to produce one carat of diamond, we have unceremoniously written off yards of shelving and consigned thousands of hours of ignoble professorial study to the dustbin.

What's left is the essence of business theory. Only 200 pages and that's all you need to know. Because theory really has no legitimate place in the high-flier's hangar. It is the oddball uncle who is invited to Christmas only because he has to be, who knows the recipe for the best turkey stuffing in the world but won't put his finger up the bird's bottom, and who doesn't laugh at jokes from cheap crackers because they aren't funny. Theory misses the point.

That's why the emphasis of this book is on practical decision-making, using realistic case studies as examples. If N-Dimensional Securities Hyperplanes are the bag you're into, put this book back on the shelf and go shopping for one of those heavyweight hardbacks with lots of serious-looking charts on the cover.

It'll cost you £25.00 but, hey, at that price, it's got to be useful, right ?

We've also taken a long hard look at the business skills which orthodox management courses overlook : the specifics of 'CV Expansion', the proper techniques for shaking hands, defensive and offensive telephone techniques, office politics, and other essentials.

We suggest that you read the book carefully, complete all the quizzes, and practise the techniques described whenever possible. To make your expectations more realistic, we strongly urge you to simulate the classroom experience used at top business schools : buy five or six additional copies of the book for friends, make up nameplates for everybody, and discuss the cases during office lunch hours. If you can't persuade your friends to do this, buy the extra copies anyway, and simulate the exercise playing each of the different roles yourself. You'll find it as rewarding as we ~~will~~ did.

Above all, keep working at it until you can exude total self-confidence when discussing any number of business issues — even those about which you know nothing. After all, it's often said that the mark of highfliers is that they are often wrong, but seldom in doubt.

BUSINESS APTITUDE TEST

Before you begin your high-flier's training, it is vital to find out whether you have an aptitude for business.

If you're the sort of person who immediately apologises when someone sneezes in your face on the tube, you probably lack the necessary self-assertion for the dog-eat-dog world of commerce. If you buy sponges for £2 off doorstep hawkers, when the same product could be had in Woolies for 75p, you *certainly* lack the financial acumen necessary for survival. And if you have the sort of mean look that makes people think you're about to offer them the leading export commodity of Bogota, all sorts of difficulties will present themselves in your business career, however honourable your intentions.

The answer is to know your limitations before you start. That way, if you clearly have no aptitude, you can avoid a business career altogether, and hopefully make a living in some non-commerical area.

But how *can* you know your limitations before you've started ? Well, you could work your way through one of the countless self-assessment books on the subject, or pay £400 to a professional adviser for a day's counselling. Alternatively, you can take our test, which is shorter and a lot cheaper. Just answer the questions below and use the points system at the end to find out whether you've got a business brain that could slice marshmallow, or a business brain *made of* marshmallow.

1. In general, you view business as :

(a) Exhilirating — an absolute blast.

(b) Character-building — but the best part of the day is the journey home and the Bloody Mary when you get there.

(c) An amusing way to kill time. Where else could you make twenty copies of your novel for nothing, or play Flight Simulator V on a full-colour screen ?

(d) A bummer. If the Social Security rules weren't so hard on free spirits you'd still be at Glastonbury.

2. You regard making money as :

    (a) The root of all evil.
    (b) Simply a harmless way to keep score.
    (c) A skill you and Bill Gates were born with.
    (e) An aphrodisiac.

3. In choosing a company to work for, which factors are the most important to you ?

    (a) The opportunity for satisfaction and personal growth.
    (b) A high drinks-party recognition factor.
    (c) Money, cash, dough, dosh, wad, scratch . . . in that order.
    (d) The best pensions plan and most liberal sick-leave policy.

4. Of the following millionaires, whose personality and achievements do you find most compelling ?

    (a) A.M. Sugar
    (b) H.M. Hefner
    (c) J.R. Ewing
    (d) R. Biggs

5. When you played Monopoly as a child, your strategy was to :

    (a) Buy the stations, collect the rent, and aim for prudent cash flow.
    (b) Borrow to the hilt to put hotels on Mayfair and Park Lane.
    (c) Make sure you looked after the bank so that you could exercise "special drawing rights" on the till if necessary.
    (d) Fly into a rage if you were wiped out, screaming "It's a filthy capitalist game anyway !"

6. Your idea of a great development at the office is :

    (a) A box of staples spilling into the guts of the photocopier at 9.15
    (b) A committee decision to upgrade from instant to filter coffee.
    (c) Being told to do a sixty-page report on the Purchase Order system.
    (d) A Post-it Note from the MD challenging you to beat the firm record for the number of weekends worked in one month.

7. During idle moments you fantasise about :

    (a) Dropping out of the rat race to become a roadie for Madonna

    (b) Having offices on five continents before you're 40.

    (c) Mounting a hostile takeover bid for Hanson plc.

    (d) Joining a firm of insolvency practitioners so you wouldn't have to worry about any more idle moments.

8. Which of the following tasks would make you feel most uncomfortable ?

    (a) Making a loyal subordinate redundant.

    (b) Asking for a pay rise.

    (c) Being asked to contribute to the cost of a leaving present for *yet another* temporary secretary in your department.

    (d) Justifying your new £300 Italian leather and mahogany-armed 'Ambassador' chair to the accounts department.

9. What image comes to mind when you look at the ink blot below :

    (a) The Jackson-Pollock in the Chairman's outer office.

    (b) A deadly insect.

    (c) A possible new packaging idea.

    (d) Prefer not to comment without first clearing it with legal.

10. When you were a child, you experienced lust in the presence of :

(a) Your parent of the opposite sex.
(b) Your parent of the same sex.
(c) Either parent's briefcase.
(d) Your Great Dane Chewy.

11. Your very first earnings came

(a) As a reward for getting straight A's in your 'O' levels.
(b) Cutting grass, shoveling snow, and distributing papers.
(c) By post, when you got in early on a chain-letter scheme.
(d) Distributing grass, cutting snow and rolling papers.

12. Your average lunch break consists of :

(a) Mystery-meat in the firm's subsidised cafeteria.
(b) A quick game of squash and a cup of low-fat yoghurt.
(c) A trip to the vending machine.
(d) Three Martinis and a strip sirloin served by waiters better dressed than you are.

13. Overall, you think your salary is :

(a) Paltry, considering what you do for your company.
(b) Stratospheric, considering what you do for your company.
(c) Embarrassing — you're only twenty-seven and you're already making twice as much as your old man.
(d) Embarrassing — you're already twenty-seven and you're only making twice as much as your old man.

14. Which of the following traits do you consider to be most critical to business success ?

(a) A finely-tuned analytical mind.
(b) The ability to get along with people.
(c) The ability to lie like a politician.
(d) An inborn ability to inherit money.

QUIZ ANSWERS

1. (a) 7 (b) 4 (c) 2 (d) 0
2. (a) 0 (b) 1 (c) 6 (d) 12
3. (a) 3 (b) -4 (c) 11 (d) -1
4. (a) 9 (b) 3 (c) 15 (d) -5
5. (a) 6 (b) 8 (c) 16 (d) 0
6. (a) 1 (b) -6 (c) 4 (d) 7
7. (a) 3 (b) 9 (c) 15 (d) 2

8. (a) -4 (b) -7 (c) 5 (d) -1
9. (a) 6 (b) 3 (c) 11 (d) -2
10. (a) -1 (b) -1 (c) 26 (d) 9
11. (a) 4 (b) 8 (c) 21 (d) 19
12. (a) 3 (b) 10 (c) 47 (d) -22
13. (a) 19 (b) -6 (c) 8 (d) 16
14. (a) 5 (b) 5 (c) 3 (d) 9

YOUR SCORE

WHAT IT ALL MEANS

Between 76 and 100

Congratulations — sort of. You have truly exceptional business acumen, in the same league as Lord Weinstock or Rupert Murdoch. You are obsessed, goal-orientated, all-consumed by work, and no doubt about as much fun to be with as a pit bull with its foot caught in a food blender.

Between 51 and 75

Not bad. Most of the MDs of Footsie companies who volunteered for this test received a similar score. You have a good business brain but would be better suited to a structured career than an entrepreneurial one. Stack up the share options, convert at the right time, and you'll still make an unconscionable fortune.

Between 26 and 50

Hey — winning isn't everything. So you've got the reverse-Midas touch, but what does that matter ? There'll always be jobs where a head for business is not required— in the arts, for instance, or doing finance work in local government.

Between 0 and 25

You were born under a bad sign. Don't read any further. Gift-wrap this book, and give it to a friend.

TOOLS OF
THE TRADE

PRODUCTION

SINCE THE END OF THE LAST war, Britain's position as a manufacturing nation has eroded faster than the wheel arches of a 1976 Allegro. The record is sufficiently apparent and far too depressing to allow anything more than a brief discussion in an upbeat book like this. Suffice it to say that, where once it seemed absurd to talk of the Spanish or the Italian economies in the same breath as our own, right now the comparison seems flattering.

What has been the cause of this perpetual malaise? Were we just too exhausted in the 50's? Too complacent in the 60's? Too belligerent in the 70's? Each decade was characterised by its own mood and each mood was deeply antipathetic to the task of taking on the phoenix economies of Germany and Japan, with their dreary focus on, of all things, production.

At the root of this casual neglect is the traditional prejudice of the educated middle-classes against industry. What kind of chap wants to get involved in production, for goodness sake? Marketing, finance, P.R., sales — these are the areas for ambitious graduates, but production?

Please.

The cachet-free image which production has enjoyed over the years is reflected in the collapse of our manufacturing base to the point at which it is, according to informed observers, almost unable to compete in world markets. To most people this is fairly alarming, but in the 1980's well-respected economists argued that it really didn't matter that much, as long as our service industries like insurance, finance and tourism continued to prosper. A comforting theory — one you *wanted* to believe — and within a whisker of being credible when those areas were prospering. But now? In the 90's ? — when you can spend all morning in Harrods Food Hall without even hearing a Texan accent ? Those gauche Americans in their yellow pants and pale blue golfing caps don't seem quite so vulgar now.

In the teeth of this crisis, what efforts has your average executive in finance, marketing, sales or personnel been making to understand production ? Well, it's not as bad as it could be. Peak-hour documentaries featuring industrial genius and all-round good guy Sir John Harvey-Jones have lifted the profile of industry a bit, and our research suggests that the average executive has quite a detailed understanding of manufacturing, best illustrated by the diagram on the adjacent page.

If you want to be a high-flier, however, your understanding of the production process needs to be *more detailed still* — even if you plan on being a merchant banker, far removed from the oily rags of industry.

Why ? At some point, you are bound to be thrown into a meeting dominated by production people. If you aren't familiar with the lingo in which the discussion is conducted, they'll sense it, and they'll pounce on you in the same way that wild animals drag down the sick members of their herd. Production people take a lot of flak; they don't waste the few chances they have to hand some back.

Filling in the Black Box

The all-purpose buzzword for conversations about production is *flow*. Flow describes how materials, labour, equipment, and energy move within the black box to produce any finished product from paper clips to spaceships. Flow can be continuous, as in the *assembly line*; intermittent, as in *batch processing*; or at a snail's pace, as in *job shop* .

1. Job Shop
Job shop is the preferred method of organisation for one-off products. Its key advantage is flexibility. Take that Aston Martin DB6 you've just got hold of down to your local mechanic, and he can do practically anything for you — bash out a dent in the front wing, remount the rear bumper, change the plates and respray for forward-shipping to Amsterdam, whatever.

Other classic job shop products are : A Savile Row suit, cosmetic surgery, legal advice, Henry Moore sculptures. The more perceptive of you will notice that all these products have one other thing in common apart from their method of production : cost

2. Assembly Line
The assembly line is the best method

NON PRODUCTION EXECUTIVE'S CONCEPTION
OF THE PRODUCTION PROCESS

INPUT:
Steel, glass,
paint, labour,
energy

OUTPUT:
Cars

FACTORY

of organisation for mass-produced items. Standardise the product, the reasoning goes, and you can standardise the production process, thus reducing unit cost. The key disadvantage of assembly line production is its lack of flexibility : if a worker takes time off to blow his nose, your new Jag arrives without a rear brake light. But in general the division of labour makes workers very efficient at their tasks because they perform them thousands of times a day. You can imagine how satisfying it is too.

Examples of assembly line products are televisions, computers, hi fi units and Stock Aitken & Waterman hits.

3. Batch Processing

Batch processing is a hybrid between job shop and the assembly line. It is the best method for producing a small number of similar items, and the flow tries to parallel as closely as possible orders that have actually been received. A good example of batch processing is the way in which Big Macs are produced in a Mcdonalds restaurant. The idea is to group things together and send them through the 'factory' as a unit, hence gaining some of the benefit of the assembly line process without a total loss of flexibility. It is a compromise solution, and there are drawbacks, as anyone who has asked for a Big Mac without gherkin on a busy Saturday lunchtime will know.

There are several other terms that are important in understanding production :

Capacity : the number of units per hour, day or year that a factory process can produce, or the number of pints that a factory worker can consume in his lunch hour.

Bottleneck : If tube travellers exit from Knightsbridge Underground at the rate of 200 a minute, and the four exit turnstiles can process only 75 tickets a minute you immediately create a traffic problem. You also create perfect conditions for the Chilean pickpockets working the Piccadilly Line. In production terminology, this is known as a 'critical bottleneck' although Tube travellers have been known to use less technical terms.

Balance : A production engineer's idea of catching "the perfect wave", balance is achieved when all bottlenecks have been removed from the production process. To return to the Underground analogy, it makes little sense to have trains arriving at Knightsbridge tube every two minutes if the passengers get crushed against the same four turnstiles every morning. It is far more sensible to achieve balance by (a) reducing the number of trains so that they arrive at 75 minute intervals, and (b) increasing the number of turnstiles to fifty-three. The Northern Line has already implemented the first part of this two-point plan.

Production in the 1990's

You have just completed the basic course in production. Don't assume, however, that the principles just expounded are only applicable to the factory environment. Increasingly, they are being applied to service businesses, with striking improvements in efficiency and profit margins. Read the following case for a hands-on look at how production techniques are being successfully applied to a non-traditional mass-production business — the restaurant.

THE FEEDLOT

"It's all a matter of keeping the flow going. Basically, we've just taken the accepted techniques of assembly-line production out of the factory and put them into the restaurant."

This is how Barny White, proprietor of The Feedlot, Manchester's most innovative and fashionable carnivorous eaterie, explains his success.

"When I first bought this building three years ago, it was a decrepit freight yard, totally abandoned and with the roof falling in. The car park we're standing in was covered in scrap and the buildings where we now have the eating areas were due to be demolished by the council."

Company History

The Feedlot was originally conceived in the Summer of 1986 when Barny White was working as production line manager at Ford's Dagenham plant. In his twenty years with Ford, White had become a specialist in many techniques of operations research : product and workforce scheduling, just-in-time inventory control, linear programming, and T.Q.M. to name a few. His obsession with production efficiency and flow was legendary, and not something he limited to the workplace. He would often find himself getting irritated by the wasteful inefficiency of other sectors of the economy, particularly the restaurant trade :

> *"I always got the impression that waiters weren't waiting on me; I was waiting on them"*

At the age of 64, White began mulling over what he was going to do after retiring from Ford. He decided to combine his interest in food with his production experience and start a completely new restaurant concept. In searching for a site, he remembered the abandoned wharves on Merseyside which he had frequently driven by on his way to meetings up there. After selling his house and drawing out nearly £75,000 in pensions benefits, he won a restoration grant from the Borough and set about renovating the site.

Using the techniques of standardisation and mass production which he had learned during his automotive career, White designed the Feedlot to correct many of the traditional flaws he saw in the restaurant business. Among his innovative ideas now up and running at the Feedlot :

- Customers are greeted on arrival by the restaurant's Inventory Control Officer, who matches parties into exact batches of forty-two. After being assigned a batch number, each party then proceeds to the restaurant's enormous bar — "The Trough" — which serves as an inventory-holding area. The Inventory Control Officer gives each batch between eighteen and twenty-two minutes at The Trough — an amount calculated to encourage consumption of no less and no more than two drinks. (More than two drinks made customers hard to round up.) The four-minute leeway is important because it allows The Trough to act as an inventory buffer against minor variances in downstream dining-room through-put.

- When the Dining-Room Manager signals to the Inventory Control Officer that he is ready to process another batch, the Control Officer takes the microphone and calls out "Batch Eighty-four, head 'em up and move 'em out ! Proceed to Dodge City !" The six Feedlot dining-rooms each hold 210 customers, and are named after famous cattle stations in the Wild West. White insists that the folksy Wild West image should permeate every aspect of the restaurant, and regards it as entirely appropriate for his waiters to slap slow diners on the rear with their stetsons to keep things moving along.

- Long, narrow tables installed in the dining-room hold a standard batch of forty-two diners (see Figure 1). Because the number of aisles between tables and the elbow space per diner is minimal, the Feedlot avoids the industry's perennial problem of wasting precious seating space by having a party of three occupy a table for six.

- The Feedlot's menu is limited to prime Scotch steaks cooked three ways : rare, medium-rare and well-done. The large forty-two person batch size allows White to estimate the exact mix of customer orders with a 95% confidence level. This means that the kitchen can start broiling the steaks even before the diners have arrived, and results in a significant reduction in customer-idle time, as well as improved customer through-put.

- The most radical innovation of all is the price : a flat £7.00 for salad, bread roll, two alcoholic drinks, and a steak. The limited menu and the high-volume turnover allows White to have his meat trucked down direct from Aberdeen by the container-load. A computer-controlled dispenser feeds the steaks direct from the back of the container into a continuous-flow broiler, automatically cooking the meat to the desired degree. From the broiler, the steaks are deposited onto numbered plates using sorting technology developed by DHL. Wastage is negligible, and because the product is hardly touched by human hand (except the diners', who are encouraged to do without cutlery) the labour cost in the kitchen is cut to the bone.

The Current Situation

After the first two years in operation, White could take great pride in the success of his new business and his contributions to restaurant science. Trade magazines profiled him as the natural

FIGURE 1
FLOW CHART OF FEEDLOT PROCESS

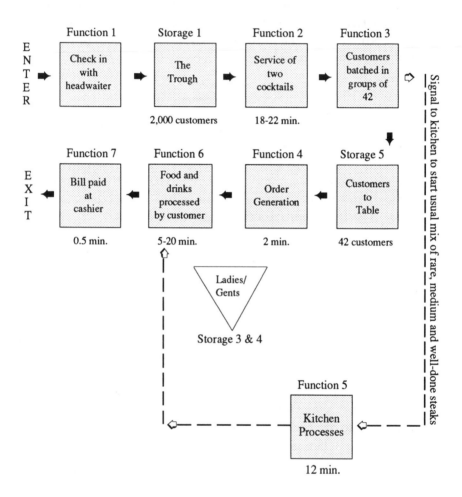

successor to Ray Kroc, and he had been asked on several occasions to give guided tours of back-room operations to Japanese restaurateurs interested in replicating the concept.

White, however, was far from complacent about his system. With average through-put time reduced to thirty-eight minutes door-to-door, and incredibly tight timing tolerances, it was always vulnerable to unexpected bottlenecks. Even a brief mechanical failure in the kitchen's cooking lines would create near stampede in The Trough, and it soon became clear that the waiters needed to do more than shout 'Yee-hah' and slap customers with their stetsons when that happened. As a short-term solution, White decided to equip his waiters with electric cattle prods — not popular with the customers, but undeniably effective when things got out of hand. (And, as White said, entirely consistent with the restaurant's theme.)

There were also occasional customers who objected to the Feedlot's methods of ensuring uninterrupted process flow. Most of these complaints centred around the waiters' habit of rubbing down the tables with dilute spirits of ammonia if they lingered beyond the thirty-eight minute deadline. Again, the cattle prods proved their worth.

White was never really happy with the cattle prods though, for obvious reasons: he was a systemist, and he wanted a solution to the bottleneck problem which was *part* of the system, rather than an external addition. After considerable study, he came up with three long-term solutions, as follows:

1. Further Mechanisation

This idea would involve the introduction of a revolving conveyor system onto which the dining tables and benches would be bolted. Customers would get straight into their seats on leaving The Trough, and would be carried all the way through the eating process by the conveyor, and automatically deposited at the exit after thirty-eight minutes.

This continous-flow system would yield a higher through-put than the current batch-processing since the conveyor could always be speeded up or slowed down as required by the backlog in The Trough. No need for batching, and goodbye cattle prods. Estimated Cost: £200,000

2. Extra Cooking Capacity

Because the usual cause of a backlog in the system was delay in the automatic cooking line, White was considering adding an extra computer-controlled broiler in the kitchen. He recognised that this £50,000 machine would stand idle most of the time, but because the Feedlot's peak capacity was over 2000 customers per hour, at an average profit of £0.83, he was confident that the investment could be recouped in bottleneck avoidance.

3. Group Price Incentives

Under this plan, the maitre d' would be given responsibility for declaring a 'capacity alert' if the crush in The Trough ever became intolerable. The crush would be deemed intolerable if it infringed EC regulations governing road transport of livestock —French interpretation. During such alerts, management would announce over the tannoy that batch price incentives were in operation. Thus for each minute *under thirty-eight* that a batch finished eating, the entire batch would be given a five pence rebate on the standard £7 price. White felt that by enlisting peer pressure, this manoeuvre could lower average cycle time to twenty-three minutes.

Questions for Discussion

1. Whch factor has contributed most to the Feedlot's success ?

(a) Low price, combined with consistent standards
(b) Its evocative Mid-Western theme
(c) Electric cattle prods

2. Which of the three options should Mr White take ?

MARKETING

"BUILD A BETTER MOUSETRAP and the world will beat a path to your door — or so the story goes. These days, having a good product is of secondary importance to having a well-financed and carefully-planned marketing campaign. Tacky products sell squillions if correctly pitched; mould-breaking products without big budgets sink without trace. Advertising, packaging, hype, merchandising — all these elements have to work in parallel to support the product, and if one of them is missing or poorly implemented, the whole enterprise lurches off balance.

The first and most important marketing decision is what to call your product. The large multinationals spend fortunes instructing consultancies to find the right name for their new products and, in some cases, to re-christen their old ones. This is not just idle tinkering: the difference between a good name and a bad name is almost as important as the difference between a good and a bad product. 'Hovis' probably wouldn't be the household name it is if it was still called 'Smith's Patent Germ Flour'. 'Post-It' notes might never have caught on at all if the manufaturer hadn't wisely truncated its full name — Minnesota Mining and Mineral Co — to the much more memorable '3M'.

Equally, a name which is bad *ab initio*, or which becomes tarnished for one reason or another, can sometimes be terminal to the product or company it represents. It just creates the wrong "mood music" for customers. *Business Age* recently ran an article on this very point, citing as examples Ratners and Dan-Air — classic cases of brand deterioration.

In general, the secret seems to be to create at the outset, or to adopt at an opportune moment, a name that is simple, easily pronounceable, and which 'sounds right' for the product.

Sometimes, by sheer chance, the founder of the company or creator of the product has a name which fulfills all these criteria : with his harsh and alliterative second name, Mikhail Kalashnikov was just *born* to develop the world's best-selling assault rifle. There was never the *slightest doubt* that Enzo Ferrari would win the Mille Miglia from the moment he was christened. And what else, quite frankly, could Laura Ashley have done apart from design evocative floral dresses for the wives of Houston oil barons hyped up on *Brideshead Revisited*. Some things were just meant to be.

Once you've got your name, it's time to concentrate on the six P's of marketing : *P*roduct, *P*rice, *P*lacement, *P*romotion, *P*roduct Life Cycle, and *P*ositioning.

Product

Product is the "complete package" of goods or services that you are selling. The same physical piece of equipment can be sold as several different products, depending on the customers you are targeting. A standard 33 mhz 486-chip PC can either be sold as an Elonex for £1000 or with an IBM badge for 30% more.

Same product, different marketing.

Price

A marketing executive must decide whether his or her product is a "commodity" or a "brand". Commodities are homogenous products of a uniform standard, like wheat, petrol, and Jackie Collins novels. With minor variances, they can be priced only at the prevailing market rate. Brands, by contrast, are differentiated from each other. This can be accomplished by giving your toothbrush a subtly-angled head, or a moulded pair of bosoms on the handle — factors adding such undeniable value to the product as to justify a significant price premium.

Recently whole industries have been trying to turn their commodity products into brand products, funneling huge amounts of money into ludicrous advertising campaigns to that end. High on the list of shame come the banks and building societies with their ill-conceived lifestyle adverts, shot at dawn in deserted freight-marshalling yards, and accompanied by bass guitar rhythms lifted straight from Pickwick's "Kings of Rock" LP set. Anybody who switches bank accounts on the basis of such stylised flummery deserves to wait in the long lunchtime queues that those same banks are too distracted to do anything about.

Spurious brand elevation is not, however, a new phenomenon. The motor industry has been at it for years. Take a standard Austin Princess circa 1977. Add on a few hundred pounds worth of leather trim, a walnut fascia, electric windows, and a new front grille, and you have not a mere Princess but a *Vanden Plas* selling for 15% more to discriminating widowers the length and breadth of West Sussex.

Placement

What 'channels' should you use to offer and deliver your product to the targeted customer ? Traditionally most goods are sold through retail channels — which can mean anything from a market stall to a High Street chain to a department store.

In the last ten years, however, direct mail has grown exponentially, and it is now possible to feed, clothe, and entertain oneself just by browsing through catalogues and picking up the phone. This is an enormously liberating concept, particularly for the single man or woman who finds it difficult to go shopping in the conventional way : no more gratuitous advice from unimaginative shop assistants along the lines of

"The camisole looks a little tight, sir. Are you sure you don't want to try Menswear ?"

Almost as striking has been the growth in 'network marketing' which sounds sophisticated but is really as old as the hills. The pioneering products were tupperware and cosmetics, but the field has widened to include double-glazing, water filters, financial services and cults. For some obscure reason, network marketing has an image problem.

Promotion

Promotion comes in two varieties: *push* and *pull*. Push is what happens when you ask the assistant at your local hardware shop which vinyl matt he recommends and he suggests Berger rather than Dulux. Maybe he uses Berger himself. Maybe he's had a bad experience with an Old English Sheepdog. But the more likely explanation is that the Berger marketing department is offering a 30p per can incentive to hardware shops this month so that they will *push* the product.

Pull advertising pre-sells the customer before he or she walks through the door; the customer is *pulled* towards the product. This pre-sell is accomplished by massive TV and print advertising campaigns. Pull is what makes otherwise reasonable six year-olds deliver non-negotiable demands for Honey Nut Loops or Pop Tarts when their mothers are trying to *push* Bran Flakes or Muesli.

Pull is an enormously powerful concept. Media critics contend that the advertising Svengalis in W1 can sell *any* product they want to, whether it has any intrinsic worth or not. That's generally not true : a product must give at least *some* benefit to the consumer, either emotional or physiological, to pull in the punters. Over 30,000 discerning consumers obviously felt that they would get more than £6.00 worth of satisfaction when they plonked down that amount for a companionable "Pet Rock" in 1987.

Product Life Cycle

Products, like living creatures, go through a set sequence of life stages. They're born, they grow up, mature, and die. In managing products, as with people, you must first determine how mature they are.

The calculator provides a good illustration of the four basic stages of product life cycle : introductory, growth, maturity and decline. When introduced to the UK market in the early 70's, calculators could add, subtract, multiply and divide, and they cost hundreds of pounds. Some of them were so chunky, they came with wheels on. Because of the price, they sold only to a specialist market of researchers, engineers and desperate Maths students.

By 1976 — well into the growth stage — you could buy a simple four-function Sinclair for under £20. Millions of units were being sold every year.

By the early 80's the price had come down so far that the calculator was rapidly becoming the perfect Christmas stocking-filler. Nearly every schoolchild had three or four, and the only way manufacturers could differentiate their models from those of the competition was by adding sexy and irrelevant new features. Models capable of playing feeble Brahms melodies, plotting biorhythms, or doubling up as alarm clocks, appeared — and disappeared — as manufacturers attempted to maintain their share of a crowded market. The market was mature.

Since then, it has stabilised, with a regular number of units being sold each year. It has not yet reached its decline stage, though it did herald the end for another product once found in every pencil case in the land: with the arrival of the calculator, the slide rule slid no more, and for that a whole generation of schoolchildren will be forever grateful.

Positioning

Suppose you are in charge of marketing dog food. There are over 10 million pets out there, and the market is too diverse for you to be all things to all dogs. There are big dogs; there are small dogs. There are young dogs; there are old dogs. There are meat-and-potatoes dogs, and there are gourmet dogs. If you try to please everyone, you may end up pleasing no-one. Instead, you must *position* your dog food to serve a particular market segment.

Nowadays, the dog food industry is so profitable and competitive that every year the market becomes more segmented as the major players try to capture a new niche which they think they have identified. It wasn't always that way. Fifteen years ago, dry biscuit diets were considered quite adequate, although softhearted owners would occasionally supplement the meal with half a tin of Chum if their pet was thirsty.

At some indefinable point in the late 1970's, canine gastronomy went crazy. Tinned dog food suddenly started appearing in all sorts of esoteric flavours — Turkey & Rabbit, Duck & Liver, Kidney & Game — and owners were tortured with shame if they couldn't afford to give their pets these gourmet meals. Then someone had the bright idea of launching meals "specially formulated for *small* breeds", and in no time at all Friskies 'A la Carte' range became a top-selling brand. Cradle-to-grave ranges followed, and now the latest thing in the dogfood market is *healthy* food : the blurb on the side of Danes Healthmeat tins states that it is "based on the natural herbs and grasses that a dog would seek out for itself in the wild." Anyone who has actually owned a dog knows that, left to forage by itself on the local common, the last kind of smell a dog looks for is a herbal one.

The constant search for new sectors is an inescapable fact of modern marketing, but there is always the danger that consumers will react against segmentation. Witness what has happened in the shampoo market : from 1985 to 1991 the trend was for shampoos and conditioners to be sold as two different products in a single range — Timotei shampoo, and Timotei Conditioning Rinse, for instance. The thrust of the advertising was that you couldn't have one without the other but (and here's the catch), you couldn't have one *with* the other because they were sold in separate bottles. For the most part, consumers bought the story, and bought the separate products.

So lucrative was this wheeze that everybody wanted a part of it, and soon the shelves were creaking with all sorts of sub-segments of this basic shampoo-conditioner division: shampoos for men, conditioners for women, shampoos for fine hair, conditioners for greasy hair, shampoos for blondes with lank hair, conditioners for bald brunettes with dandruff... you name it, the marketing people got to work on it with a new bottle, a new label, and the same old detergent.

And then, suddenly, Vidal Sassoon blew the gaff with their Wash-n-Go Range — a shampoo that *also acts as a conditioner*. No need to buy them separately, because Wash-n-Go cleans *and* conditions. It does both jobs in one go! No need to buy two separate bottles any more !

The old two-bottle scam is by no means dead, but it was badly winded. Other brands claiming multi-functional properties quickly appeared on the market (the most bizarre being *Finesse*, specially formulated, apparently, to detect which parts of your scalp need a lot of conditioner and which don't need any. Now that's an intelligent conditioner.)

Everyone in the industry *knew* that sooner or later there would be a backlash against the separate shampoo and conditioner standard. The only question was who would spoil the party first, and when. In the end, it was Proctor & Gamble, itself an owner of numerous separates, that led the field with its Vidal Sassoon range.

The lesson to be learned from this story is that product positioning constantly has to be reviewed in the light of changing market conditions. The stubborn "We've always made 'em this way, and we don't intend to change things now" attitude may work for the Morgan Car Company, but for most products it's the quickest way to oblivion.

That completes the basic graduate-level course in marketing. Now turn the page for a hands-on look at how one company positioned its new product in a particularly competitive market.

'NATURAL STAINES'

It was a lovely Spring day in West Drayton. John Black looked out of his third-floor office window and peered at the high banks of the Staines Reservoir in the distance. Then, sighing, he turned back to the group of six senior executives sitting across the table. He managed a wry smile: "There it is, ladies and gentlemen," he said, pointing at the reservoir, "*Source Staines*". He leaned back in his chair. "We have less than six months to go before your advertising agency begins the official launch for Natural Staines , and we still have not decided on a final marketing plan for the product."

Company History

The West Drayton Soft Drinks Company Ltd was founded in 1923 by Nathan Schwartz, who got into the business when he invented a new way of bottling carbonated water. Over the next forty-five years the company built up its range of products and its turnover to the point at which, in 1969, it had a 41% share of the take-home soft drinks trade in the South East.

Unfortunately, it could not maintain its position. In the early 1970's, heavyweights like Schweppes and Allied Lyons, taking advantage of their ability to afford national advertising campaigns and to invest in the latest and most efficient bottling technology, began underpricing WDSF and driving it out of the market. They also took advantage of an unfortunate change in WDSF's management (see Figure 1). Suddenly, and catastrophically, the company's market share went on the slide as its main product range — Koala Sodas — began to look outdated and overpriced. (They had always tasted ghastly, but that had never been a problem.) By 1991 the bottling division sales were down to £2.1 million against their 1958 peak of £6 million.

In early 1991, John Black, grandson of the company's founder, was asked by his grandmother to leave his job at United Biscuits and take the helm of the ailing family company. His first thought, on accepting the job, was that he should spend eight months papering over the cracks and then hive it off to whoever was willing to have it. That way, the family would at least emerge with some capital intact.

That's exactly what would have happened if he hadn't tuned in, purely by chance, to a documentary comparing the health properties of various spring and mineral waters with those of ordinary London tap water. What Black saw completely changed his strategy for WDSF. The researchers had taken samples from all the top branded waters and another from the tap, and analysed them for potassium, sodium and bacterial content. Incredibly, ordinary tap water came out favourably, whereas all of the top brands — sold in part on their health properties — had levels higher, in one respect or another, than recommended in EC regulations.

Even more significant, from WDSF's point of view, was the fact that in blind *tasting* of fifty-one waters, good old London Brown came a respectable 7th out of 26 waters tested. So not only was it safe; it also tasted yummy. And where does London water come from ? Staines Reservoir, that's where — the same source used by WDSF for the basic ingredient in its Koala soft drinks.

Suddenly, Black realised that, with a little business shimmy, WDSF could move out of the terminally-unprofitable soft drinks market into the licence-to-print-money world of bottled water. With a new bottle shape, a new name, a bit of advertising, and a smart label, the company could re-jig its Raspberry Soda — now dying at 36p a bottle — and sell it for the Perrier-rivalling price of 69p. The cost of the product itself would be lower than the sodas, as they wouldn't even have to buy the fruit flavourings.

FIGURE 1: PRODUCTIVITY LIFE CYCLE FOR SCHWARTZ/BLACK FAMILY

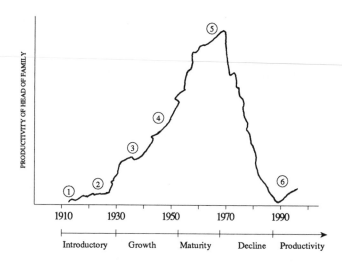

1. Nathan Schwartz, founder of the West Drayton Soft Drinks Company arrives in London with 26 Hungarian pengos in his pocket. Saves £2,000 in ten years selling ice to up-market restaurants.

2. While preparing for his morning rounds, Schwartz accidentally drops a piece of ice into a horse's water bucket and notices release of CO_2. Patents "revolutionary" carbonation process and founds WDSF to market his invention.

3. Saturates West London with product, and gradually gains foothold in wider market by pitching product as a patent medicine during the great swine flu epidemic in 1937.

4. Nathan's son, Jacob Schwartz, finishes his accountancy exams and takes control of company as his father goes into retirement (1946). Begins market-ing product in new bottle and investing in the brand — now called Koala Sodas. Turnover increases 30% p.a. for 15 years.

5. Jacob's son, Elliot Black, graduates from Oxford with PPE degree. Spurns job working for WDSF and takes publishing job with Hodders. Reluctantly takes control of WDSF on untimely death of father (1967), and moves head office to Mayfair. Elected to Boards of London Philharmonic (1971) and Tate Gallery (1973).

6. John Black, Elliot's son, is brought in by his grandmother, Rose Schwartz (1991). Mandate: to rescue WDSF from the clutch of his dilettante father. An MBA from Cranfield, and veteran of four years at United Biscuits, Black begins revamping company operation with launch of 'Natural Staines' brand.

Black could hardly contain his excitement. He grabbed the phone and buzzed his secretary. "Sarah, you know those Bacardi advertisements you see on television," he said, "Find out who makes them. We're going into the fashion business."

The Advertising Agency's Analysis

At John Black's request, Josh Abbott, senior account manager at Osborne, Perkins and Canzonelli, implemented a three-month £30,000 market research study to analyse the bottled water market as it existed in July 1991. The brief was to determine whether it was viable for WDSF to enter the bottled water market.

After reviewing the Report's conclusions, the directors of WDSF agreed to go ahead with the new product, penciling in the Autumn of 1992 as a launch date. The first consideration was where to position the product, since this would dictate all other decisions: its name, its price, the bottle and label design, and so on. Black knew from his days at United Biscuits that it would be suicidal to take on a dominant market leader like Perrier head-to-head. There would have to be some differentiation, a USP, for the WDSF water if it was to have any chance of breaking into the market. There were really only two options:

(1) To position it as a water equal in quality to Perrier but at a lower price, or;

(2) To go for the high ground and actually position it *above* Perrier at an even more inflated price.

After weighing up the pros and cons, Black ruled out the budget approach. Distribution costs for bottled drinks were notoriously high and to be commercially viable, a discount brand would have to be selling in the sort of huge quantities only achieved by the supermarket own-labels. (He rejected an interesting suggestion by his marketing director — that they should imitate Pepsi and Coca Cola by selling the product as a concentrate which could be diluted to full strength by regional bottlers using their local tap water.)

He decided instead to position the water in the hitherto un-charted super-premium sector where, he believed, customers would pay £1.30 upwards for a 70cl bottle. After all, look what they pay for Aqua Libra.

Having decided on its positioning, the directors' thoughts imme-diately turned to consideration of the product's name. A brainstorm-ing session yielded a name which they all felt reflected both the purity of the product and its geographical origin — 'Natural Staines'.

The Advertising Campaign

Wednesday, 24th May 1992 — D-day. The directors of WDSF sat back in their chairs as the advertising agency presented three storyboards outlining possible approaches for the ad. campaign. The agency believed that each approach would give the water the image of prestige and purity necessary to justify a price £0.20 higher than Perrier's. The approaches were :

1. The Elitist Approach, designed to appeal to up-market con-sumers seeking identification with the finer things in life.

2. The Patriotic Approach, designed to appeal to those millions of consumers who nurse a secret guilt about buying French water when *they* won't buy our lamb.

3. The Diet Approach, positioning the water as a low-calorie beverage, to appeal to a market segment that, in the absence of specific advertising, might not realise that Perrier has no calories either.

Leaning forward and cleaning his glasses, Black signalled to Josh Abbott, the account manager, to go through the storyboards one more time.

STORYBOARD 1: NATURAL STAINES WATER —
The Elitist Approach

1. (A panorama of the London skyline at night. Resonant voice-over by Alan Whicker:) "If you travel a lot, like I do, you learn to appreciate home. Now, from the greatest city in the world, comes the greatest water in the world . . . ."

2. (A model's hand pours the water from its bottle into a heavy crystal glass, dramatically lit. Voice-over continues:)
" . . . . Natural Staines water !"

3. (A shot of Staines Reservoir at dusk, with a striking pink sunset photographically super-imposed. Voice-over continues:)
"Direct to <u>you</u> from Source Staines, alive with sparkle and flavour."

Client: West Drayton Soft Drinks
Agency: Osborne, Perkins and Canzonelli

4. (A shot of an elegant couple emerging from their Mercedes in front of Langan's Brasserie. Voice-over continues:)
"Long the water of the Grosvenors, the de Waldens, and now Michael Caine . . . . "

5. (A close-up of the bottle. Voice-over continues:)
" . . . Natural Staines water, the essence of our capital city, is now available to you across the country, bottled with natural sparkle by the people of London."

6. (Camera pans back to the bottle being held by Michael Caine as he sits at a table in Langan's. Voice-over continues:) "Natural Staines. It may cost a little more . . . but at Source Staines we sell no water before its time."

STORYBOARD 2: NATURAL STAINES WATER —
The Patriotic Approach

1. (Panorama of a ship in dock, with a crane lifting a VW Golf onto the harbourside. In the foreground, an amiable stevedore, carrying a wooden crate, speaks to the camera:) "Working on the docks gives a man a big thirst for the good things in life . . ."

2. (Zoom in on stevedore, carrying a crate with 'PERRIER' stamped on the side) "Every day, I handle goods from all over the world — Swiss watches, Italian clothes, Russian caviar — but there's one imported product I can't understand — French bottled water."

3. (He puts down the crate, opens it with a crowbar, pulls out a bottle of Perrier, takes a swig, then spits it out in disgust.) "Believe me, I've tried them all. Thank goodness we've now got a world-beating water of our own — Natural Staines!

Client: West Drayton Soft Drinks
Agency: Osborne, Perkins and Canzonelli

4. (He sits down on the Perrier crate, puts a packed lunch-box on his lap, and takes out a bottle of Natural Staines) "That's why my wife always packs my lunch-box with something a little bit special — a cool refreshing bottle of Natural Staines."

5. (He gets up and begins hammering the top back on the Perrier crate.) "As far as I'm concerned, the French can keep their water. But Natural Staines, with the red, white and blue label, is **ours**." We close in on his face as he takes another sip of Natural Staines. "It's too good to share."

6. (Camera pans back to panorama of the dock. Stevedore yells to his boss:) "Hey, Terry, this crate's damaged!" (He turns to the camera and winks.)

STORYBOARD 3: NATURAL STAINES WATER —
The Diet Water Approach

1. (Shot of Burt Reynolds on King's Road ogling an appoaching blonde. Burt's voice-over:) "Wow, what a body!"

2. (Burt's head swivels as the blonde walks by him. Voice-over continues:) "My friends in the States are always asking me why the women in London have such great figures . . . "

3. (Close-up of Burt, still on the King's Road. Speaking, intimately, to camera:) "Know what I tell them ?"

Client: West Drayton Soft Drinks
Agency: Osborne, Perkins and Canzonelli

4. (Burt is now sitting down at an outdoor café — maybe a Dome, or Cafe Rouge)
" . . . . it's the water. That's right, the delicious, no-calorie water of West London."

5. (A close-up of a bottle of Natural Staines. Voice-over continues:) "Now bottled at *Source Staines*, Natural Staines Lite is the first bottled water as light as its name."

6. (Camera pans back to show Burt sharing the table with the same blonde seen earlier)
"No-calorie Natural Staines Lite." (She pats his taut stomach. He glances down. Then he looks up at the camera and says:) "Want to know another secret?" (He smiles, as if the cat's out of the bag, and whispers to camera:) "I drink it too."

Questions for Discussion

1. Which of the three possible advertising approaches do you think would penetrate the bottled water market most rapidly ?

2. How do you think the product would sell best in London — in bottles, or on tap ?

FINANCE

"NEITHER A BORROWER NOR a lender be" wrote the Bard. Six years ago, when individual and corporate credit was easy to come by, and business optimism ran high, his advice might reasonably have been dismissed as over-cautious and 400 years past its sell-by date.

The great business figures of the 1980's were all making it on other people's money, and shareholders who went along for the ride benefited handsomely. Okay, so the ride got a little bumpy later on, and shareholders in some companies were taken for a ride in a very different sense, but if you got your timing right, there were rich pickings to be had.

Contrast with the 90's : blip, slump, recession, depression — whatever technical term you want to give it — the current state of the economy has imposed an edge-of-seat existence on the majority of businessmen. Survival is the name of the game, and companies still around to testify have discovered that credit is a two-edged sword — a weapon as likely to gash one's own jugular as to smite one's competitiors.

With blood running thick in the streets, the defeated have turned angrily on their bankers — once midwives of their ambitions, now more like corporate undertakers (with an unhealthy interest in euthanasia) — and heaped criticism upon them for (a) lending too freely when times were good, and (b) withdrawing credit when borrowers need it most.

So was the Bard right ? Is business success best ensured by a debt-free balance sheet ? Can lenders be trusted to behave in anything other than their own short-term interest when the going gets tough ?

As an academic matter, it's an interesting point — though not for this book. As a practical matter, growing businesses cannot realistically do without credit. If you doubt this, consider the following scenario:

You are a moonshiner from Carnoustie, distilling whisky on the black market. Fed up with the hassle, and keen to be bought out by Guinness, you decide to go legit. Instead of selling your product within days of it being produced, you now have to age it for at least eight years to make it acceptable to discerning consumers.

The cash flow implications are quite serious. You have to buy your yeast, wood for the still, and two hundred charred casks *now*, and you have to run your distillery for eight full years, without receiving a penny in revenue. You won't actually have a product to sell until the beginning of the next millenium.

The only way you're going to survive is to borrow enough money to keep you going for those eight years. Assuming you are able to borrow £400,000, paying £100,000 or so in accumulated interest, the projections would look like this :

Income :	£800,000
Expenses	— £400,000
Interest	— £100,000
PROFIT	£300,000

In other words, you'd have made £300,000 entirely through the use of O.P.M. This is known as 100% leverage.

CASH FLOW OF CARNOUSTIE WHISKY DISTILLERY

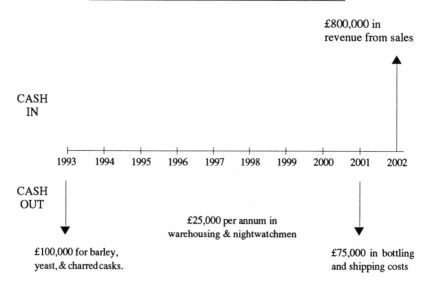

£800,000 in
revenue from sales

CASH
IN

1993 1994 1995 1996 1997 1998 1999 2000 2001 2002

CASH
OUT

£25,000 per annum in
warehousing & nightwatchmen

£100,000 for barley,
yeast, & charred casks.

£75,000 in bottling
and shipping costs

Unfortunately, life is rarely so kind. Bankers don't like to fight on the front lines : if something goes wrong, they want their money out first. As a result, most businesses are required to come up with at least 50 per cent of the money in the form of equity. Let's assume you find a partner to put up £200,000, and agree to give him half the profits. The deal now looks like this :

Income :	£800,000
Expenses	— £400,000
Interest	— £50,000
GROSS PROFIT	£300,000
Less dividend to father-in-law	—£150,000
Profit left for you	£150,000

Still a good deal, but not nearly as attractive as before : your partner demands a greater return for his investment than the bank does, because he knows he's sucking on hind tit.

The trick in deciding how to finance the company is to achieve "optimum capital structure" by finding the right mix of risky debt and expensive equity. Debt may be cheap but remember — if the public starts to develop a liking for rum during the eight years that your single malt is maturing, the bank still expects to be paid on time, whereas your father-in-law can wait.

So much for the basics of finance. Now we can move on to more advanced quantitative concepts in which the maths is a little more challenging but for which the rewards of mastery are that much greater.

LESSON 1

Mergers & Acquisitions

Principle : 1 + 1 = 3

Nothing excites the financial community so much as when one large company tries to take over another. Such bids generate huge fees for accountants, lawyers, banks, advertising agencies, and P.R. companies. They stimulate turnover on the stock market from which brokers make their money. And, best of all, they generate these rewards whether or not the bid succeeds.

It follows that many mergers and acquisitions are not conceived, planned and executed by the parties themselves, but by the coterie of advisers that surround the companies and who stand to benefit from the deal. In short, some eager-beaver 26-year old in a merchant bank is told to go out and find a deal to put to the client, and spends the next two months scouring Extel cards and microfiches for a plausible fit. He knows that if he doesn't come up with something at the end of his research, the next assignment he'll be working on is his CV.

This task is not unlike panning for gold in the Yukon : it isn't the slightest bit glamorous, or remotely enjoyable, but the rewards can be spectacular. Like panning, you have to pay close attention to what you're doing, because when the proposal is presented to the client, the numbers have got to add up.

It's no use making 1 + 1 equal 2. In the world of mergers and acquisitions, 1 + 1 must equal 3 or more — that is, the value of the merged concern must be higher than the value of the two component companies separately. This is known as *synergy*.

The perverse mathematics of synergy are explained by the economies of scale from which a larger group can benefit, and by the commercial advantages which increased market share brings. You can buy raw materials cheaper, you can rationalise your sales force, marketing costs can be spread wider, and so on.

In practice, synergy is often more imagined than real, and traditional laws of mathematics have a habit of reasserting themselves almost as soon as the ink on the bid documents is dry. Rationalisation plans take, on average, about twice as long to implement as predicted in offer documents, and the expected bottom-line benefits about twice as long again. What shareholders in the combined group often end up with is a proportionately smaller holding in a group worth a traditional 2, less the monumental fees which have been paid out to various advisers.

A classic example of the Synergy Myth occurred in the mid 1980's when banks, building societies, and financial services groups spent *fortunes* buying up estate agencies all over the country. Partners with piffling two and three-branch agencies in the middle of nowhere were offered absurd sums of money to sell out to the General Accident, the Prudential or Royal Life. The explanation put forward for this wanton squandering of shareholders' money was that the agencies would, at the same time as they sold houses and flats, be able to sell mortgage policies, pensions policies, life assurance and a whole range of other financial products to the purchasers. In other words, the deals promised synergy on a grand scale.

The flaw in this plan quickly became apparent when the property market went into full-scale meltdown at the end of the 80's. Six years on,

"I'm on what you might call the sexy side of banking — project finance, asset finance, acquisition finance — that sort of thing."

many of the agencies built up at such great expense by the financial institutions have been sold off — in many cases back to the original owners for a fraction of their 1986 'value'.

LESSON 2

Demergers

Principle : $3 = 1+1+1+1$

When the rich gravy train of mergers and acquisitions dried up in the late 80's, the merchant banks had teams of highly-paid corporate fi-

nance experts twiddling their thumbs. Some of these guys were used to £100,000 a year — and that was just the bonus. They realised that if replacement business wasn't found, and quick, the only six-figure salary they'd ever see again would be one where two of the figures stood to the right of the decimal point.

They hunkered down and came up with that new business in the form of *demerger* advice. In a neat flipside to synergy theory, demerger theory rests on the principle that the whole may not be worth as much as the sum of its parts : companies can become so top-heavy and cumbersome, that it makes sense to implement a programme of corporate divorce by 'spinning off' subsidiaries as separate entities.

As with any divorce proceedings supervised by lawyers and bankers, the fees involved often make the separating parties wish they had stayed together in the first place.

LESSON 3

Perfect Market Theory

Principle : $R = ß (R\prod - R)$

Everybody knows the story of Ian McGlinn, the garage-owner who put a few thousand into Body Shop fifteen years ago, and who now struggles along on a capital investment worth £97 million. Or of Stephen Rubin who bought a large chunk of Pentland for £75,000 just as the 'trainer' revolution took off, and whose stock is now worth £240 million.

Inspired by such tales, thousands of people gamble their savings in the equities market, hoping to catch the next stock market rocket moments before its fuel tanks are ignited. Unfortunately for most investors, their search is likely to be about as successful as the centuries-old search for the Holy Grail.

Why ? Because if you want a *larger* than average slice of the cake, you've got to have your hand on the cake knife. Standing politely round the table and accepting whatever happens to come your way — the position of most private investors — will guarantee only crumbs.

This is not idle cynicism : it is backed up by rigorous research and is dogma at all major business schools. Perfect market theory states that it is *impossible* to beat the market . . . unless you're an insider and know something that other investors don't, or you are very very lucky on a consistent basis. All non-insider information, according to the theory, instantly becomes common knowledge and is already taken into account in the share price by the time you get to hear of it.

Next time you read one of those adverts for a Stock Market tip-sheet, just remember that :

(1) The tips are written at least three days before you receive your newsletter — a long time in the Stock Market.

(2) There are 20,000 other subscribers in on the same 'hot tip'.

(3) The publishers of the tip-sheet are allowed to hold shares in the stocks they tip.

In short, by the time one of those tips has got to one of us small fry, it's about as hot as a yak's trademark in a severe Himalayan winter.

THE SYNERGENE CORPORATION

Sir Ian Wolfe, founder and Chief Executive of Synergene, settled back into his plush chair, pulled a letter off his desk and studied it, then looked up and spoke: "So Mr Seager... you're in your third term at INSEAD and you want to analyse the merger. I have no problem with that, — subject to you signing the usual confidentiality undertakings — but the place to start is with the investment bankers and the pension funds, not with me. Go and speak to them, then come back and I'll tell you how we saw it this end?" With that, he stood up, indicating that Seager should leave.

The 'Merger of the 90's', as it had been touted in the financial press, had joined together two Footsie companies, each one the darling of its respective sector. The first was Brancusi Jeans, an old trading company which bought in ordinary blue jeans from mainland China, stitched the 'Brancusi' logo on the back pocket, ran advertisements of international film stars endorsing them, and raked in £120 a pair at top department stores all over the world.

The second was Geneceuticals plc, a pharmaceuticals firm specialising in recombinant DNA research. The genetic-engineering industry may still be at least five years away from making a profit, but at the time when Geneceuticals went public in 1986 no-one knew that. The company placed stock for £9 per share, putting a cool £5 million into the pocket of the company's founder — Sir Ian Wolfe.

Wolfe, however, was not the type to stop at a moderate killing like that when he sensed *serious* money in the offing. Realising that the City would be completely bowled over by the merger of a company which sold jeans for five times more than they were worth with another company which sold genetic-engineering stock for twenty times more than it was worth, Wolfe was *more* than receptive when his investment banker telephoned to flesh out the details of what he called "an interesting proposal".

The Investment Banker

Seager entered the Broadgate offices of Shaftoe Roberts, the merchant bankers who had helped Wolfe put the deal together. A female receptionist — possibly Cindy Crawford — greeted him with a disdain which both of them recognised as entirely appropriate to his station. Seager was impressed.

Taking in the sheer opulence of his surroundings — the mahogany-paneled walls, the gilt-framed oils, the neatly-laid out copies of the FT, Times and Wall Street Journal — he speculated on whether this world would ever be for him. It was a far cry from Wisley Injection Mouldings Ltd, where he had spent three hard but satisfying years before starting his M.B.A. Plush offices like these lacked the raw edge of the Nissen huts at W.I.M., but no doubt one could get used to them. The people were another matter. Would he ever gain acceptance in the world of hand-stitched shoes and two-ply poplin cuffs ? Would he be the only one in the office on the 4th of June ?

Just as Seager was reaching the conclusion that perhaps merchant banking wasn't for him, Claudia Schiffer arrived to escort him to Boardroom 27 where a fresh cup of filter coffee, black, one sugar, awaited him. (These guys knew how to do their homework.)

The managing partner adjusted his tortoiseshell glasses and began his story. "As you know Ian, the stock market has been in a highly-nervous state since 1987, turnover down, low confidence in the market, lack of foreign investment, and so on . . . I need hardly elaborate.These conditions make our job that much harder. It's just not as easy to promote a stock with a simple share split or earnings-per-share manipulation nowadays."

Seager was surprised at his candour.

"With building, motor, electronics and basic manufacturing sectors all shot to ribbons" he continued, "we have to pick our stocks very carefully on the strength of proven future prospects. About 10 months ago, one of our young corporate financiers came up with this madcap idea of combining a genetic research company and a fashion house into a single company."

He shook his head, eyes closed, in silent rapture.

"At first, no-one would even consider the proposal, but things were pretty quiet, and one Friday afternoon I decided to look it over. I loved it from the start. It was so simple. We put together one share of Geneceuticals at £28 with one of Brancusi at £6 and sold the package for £48. That, as they say, is synergy."

He lit his pipe. "We put the issue on the market, and it sold out in minutes. It was magical."

"What about the future?" asked Seager. "Are Synergene's shares a good buy now?"

"It's difficult to say" said the partner. "Things aren't what they used to be. Anyway, we won't be involved again until the companies demerge."

Seager was stunned. "You expect them to demerge?" he said.

"Well, there's no more mileage in it for us unless they do. Besides, between you and me, how much synergy can there really be between eggheads in a biology lab and a bunch of designers in Soho Square?" He smiled. " I'm led to believe there was something of a culture clash."

"But if the merger is going to be unravelled, what on earth was the point of it in the first place?"

The partner pointed to the painting of a young boy hanging on his wall. "That's a Rembrandt," he replied.

The Investor

Seager's last stop was a six-room suite of offices in an unfashionable 70's block just off Smithfield meat market. The name on the brass plate in the doorway was suitably nondescript — Samuelson Investments — and only those in the know would have realised that this was, in fact, the nerve centre of one of the country's wealthiest families.

Jeremy Samuelson, 36 year-old scion of the family billions, had bought ten per cent of Synergene in a private placement. Seager had come to ask him why.

"Well basically, when two fashionable stock market companies merge, it gives the investment community something to sell to their customers. It's such a rare event in the 90's, and in this case the synergy stories were irresistable. Salesmen were instructed to tell fund managers that Brancusi was going to get the Geneceutical scientists to create human clones of uniform size, with bums so flat that everyone — even those on the wrong side of fifty — would be able to fit into designer jeans. So, in a single generation, the sales of Brancusi would shoot up, and the other denim manufacturers would be stuck with millions of pairs of odd-sized jeans." Samuelson sipped his Cranberry & Thyme tea. "Pure science fiction, of course. They must have had Asimov on retainer."

"But you bought the stock anyway."

"We certainly did." said Samuelson. "At £36 a share, and it went on the market at £48 the next day. It's still got another £5 in it, but the fund managers will dump it before then. Anyway we sold out soon after the merger. That's why we've been successful — we've always known when to get out."

He winked. "Of course, our great advantage is that, as soon as investors hear that Samuelson has taken a major position, they reckon there *must* be something good. The share price goes up and there is something good — at least for us."

Sir Ian Wolfe

With his preliminary research complete, Seager returned to the Wolfe's office to get the summing-up. "Can I ask what it was about the merger that drew your personal interest ?" he said. "Was it just the money, or did you have an interest in the fashion industry ?"

He laughed. "Armani, Versace, *Wolfe* . . . you must be joking! No, if I was honest I'd have to say that it was the money." He paused, reflecting a minute " . . . but not *just* the money. At least as important were the humanitarian aspects of the deal."

"Humanitarian ?" said Seager, puzzled.

"Look at the results." said Wolfe. "The merchant banks and lawyers did nicely out of it — maybe a million a piece. And I got 12 per cent of the shares, now worth £40 million. Everybody benefited."

"What about the third group ?" said Seager. "What about the shareholders ?"

Wolfe thought for a moment. "Well, two out of three's not bad."

"But you didn't *do* anything," said Seager, almost losing his temper. "Why should you get something for nothing ?"

"That's how the City works, young man." said Wolfe. "If you want to feel good about what you do, join the Salvation Army."

Questions for Discussion

1. Would <u>you</u> buy shares in Synergene if you knew that its first £1 of genetic-engineering profit was not due until 1999 ?

2. What methods do you think City analysts use to price a stock issue like Synergene ?

  (a) Fundamental analysis of the potential profits of the company.
  (b) Analysis of the market's reaction to similar issues in the past ?
  (c) Hunch.
  (d) A Ouija board ?

ACCOUNTING

NO INITIATION INTO THE mysteries of business would be complete without a look at the black art of accounting, the body of theory and conventions which determines the uses and abuses to which numbers can be put. A chilled bottle of Bricourt (£15.49) and a packet of Raffles cigarettes (£1.98) seemed at first sight a fair explanation for Threshers' debiting the Chancellor's Access account with £17.47. It is part of the wonder of numbers that the reality was two bottles of non-vintage claret (£7.98) and one of Margaux 1990 (9.49).

That's why, demoralising as the prospect is, it's worth getting a handle on accounting theory. When your division's £5 million quarterly profit is transformed into a £3 million loss by an arbitrary change in the allocation of group overheads, you need to be able to show that the loss is the result of the Finance Director's whim, rather than your ineptitude.

Debits = Credits

Our basic course in accounting begins with the *yin* and *yang* of the business world : debits and credits. These can be highly confusing to the layman. Supposing you deposit £500 in your high-interest bank account. Is that a debit or a credit? Simple. It's both. To you it's a debit — which is good. The bank owes you money. But it's also a credit — which is bad, because you no longer have the money to hand.

More sophisticated analysis of whether debits and credits are 'good' or 'bad' is fraught with danger. Like people, they are often the product of their environment. So debits residing on the asset side of the balance sheet are good. Debits on the equity side are bad. If you understand that, it is to your credit — which is good. If you don't understand it, go to the top of the class anyway; the world can always use another honest accountant.

company therefore has £100 in assets — cash contributed by you as the owner.

Assets = Liabilities + Equity

The core concept of accounting is *balance*, as commonly illustrated in that forbidding document, the *balance sheet*. To gain an understanding of how a balance sheet is created and what it means, consider the following example.

Imagine you are a third-year student who spots a new business opportunity. You notice that each September all the incoming students in your college rush down to the local hardware shop and buy a toaster for their room. You also notice that, at the end of their degree, final year students nearly always flog their toasters back to the same shop at a fraction of their value. Two months later, the next batch of freshers buy these 'reconditioned' toasters virtually at list.

Armed with this information, you decide to enter the high-rolling world of toaster *arbitrage*, with the aim of doing to the campus electrical appliance market what the fat guys from Texas nearly did to the silver market.

In May, you take the last £100 out of your bank account and start a company with it, issuing yourself 100 ordinary shares, fully paid. The

ASSETS	
Cash	£100
LIABILITIES	
Shares	£100
(100 x £1 Ordinary)	

Realising that you will need more capital to corner the market, you persuade your grandmother to stump up £1500 for your venture. She agrees to do this, however, only if you guarantee her a return of 10 per cent above base rate and on condition that you provide her with a promissory note agreeing to pay back the loan at a specified future date. So sweet is the arbitrage spread, and so lukewarm the response from 3i, that

"Auditors are people who have found accountancy too exciting. Their professional task is to walk the battlefield long after the shouting is over, bayonetting the wounded."

Sir John Banham, former Director-General of the CBI, January 1993

"John, you've been our auditor for 24 years now. For the sake of a silly decimal point, let's see if we can't reach the quarter-century, hmm?"

you agree to these rapacious terms.

The balance sheet now looks like this ⇨

Working methodically and quietly, you contact every third-year student three months before the end of term, and sign contracts agreeing to buy their toasters when the course has finished.

By the end of July, you have bought up over 150 toasters at an average of £10 each. These enter your balance sheet as £1,500 worth of inventory. Of course you now have £1,500 less cash in your ac-

ASSETS	
Cash	£1,600
Total Assets	£1,600
LIABILITIES & EQUITY	
Promissory Note	£1,500
Shares (100 x £1 Ordinary)	£100
Total L& E	£1,600

count.

Your balance sheet now reads as follows :

```
                ASSETS

Cash                      £100
Inventory               £1,500

Total Assets            £1,600

        LIABILITIES & EQUITY

Promissory              £1,500
Note

Shares                    £100
( 100 x £1 Ordinary )

Total L& E              £1,600
```

Notice that both sides of the balance sheet still *balance*.

Over the summer you store the inventory in your grandmother's attic (hence complying with the rigorous inspection rights upon which she insisted). In September you stake out the campus refectory, attend every single fresher's drinks party, leaflet the entire student body, and by the end of the month you have successfully unloaded 140 of the toasters for £15 cash each, selling the other ten on credit to the University Rugby Club.

You have now sold the toasters for £2,250. Since they cost you only £1,500, you have made £750 profit. However, Only £2,100 of the sales revenue is in cash. The £150 from the ten sold on credit is recorded on the balance sheet as an *account receivable*. Thus

```
                ASSETS

Cash                     £2,200
Accounts Receivable        £150

Total Assets             £2,350

        LIABILITIES & EQUITY

Promissory               £1,500
Note

Retained                   £750
Earnings

Shares                     £100
( 100 x £1 Ordinary )

Total L& E               £2,350
```

Unfortunately, the front-row forwards who own the toasters sold on credit are showing a reluctance to part with the £150 they owe you. On two successive visits to their house, you are made an offer you can't refuse, and deem further collection efforts innappropriate. Your grandmother is anxious to assist, but after much thought you decide that your balance sheet should reflect the likelihood that you will never be paid. Kissing your accounts receivable goodbye by 'writing them down' by the £150, you reduce your earnings by a corresponding figure. The new balance sheet looks like this:

ASSETS	
Cash	£2,200
Accounts Receivable	—
Total Assets	£2,200
LIABILITIES & EQUITY	
Promissory Note	£1,500
Retained Earnings	£600
Shares (100 x £1 Ordinary)	£100
Total L& E	£2,200

Finally, it's time to pay off your grandmother's loan out of your profits. You give her back the £1,500 principal, and an additional £120 from your earnings as interest due over the six months. Your final balance sheet looks like this :

ASSETS	
Cash	£580
Accounts Receivable	—
Total Assets	£580
LIABILITIES & EQUITY	
Promissory Note	—
Retained Earnings	£480
Shares (100 x £1 Ordinary)	£100
Total L& E	£580

A quick analysis of the final balance sheet shows what kind of year you had : £480 of profit on £100 of original investment. That's a return of 480 per cent. Not bad. Maybe you could franchise the idea. Anyway, if you're making *that* kind of money, you can probably give up your accounting studies. Go out and hire Price Waterhouse.

RATIO ANALYSIS

Even experts find it difficult to interpret balance sheets and income statements at a glance. To save time, they use *ratio analysis*. Here are some quick and dirty ratios to help you translate financial statements into comprehensible form.

Ratio Title	Equation	Acceptable Range	Useful for determining ...
Payout Ratio	Chief Executive's salary / profits	No greater than 100%	CEO's expendability
Acid-test Ratio	(Current assets - inventory)/current liabilities	Greater than 1.0	Adequacy of cash level
'Hello' Ratio	No. of pages of glossy filler/total pages in Annual Report	No more than 96%	Plausibility of financial statements
Leverage Ratio	Debt/Equity	Less than 1.0	Solvency
Turnover Ratio	(Firings + hirings)/ employees	Less than 6.7	Velocity of body-rolling
Profit Margin	Profit/Sales	Less than 98%	Vulnerability to MMC or obscenity law investigation.
Ratio Alger	Founder's	Less than 50%	Advisability of marrying into founder's family.

Deciphering an Annual Report

In the old days, annual reports were printed on plain paper, and contained nothing but columns of numbers. They were produced by the Company Secretary and the Finance department, and intended only for shareholders. ICI's annual report in the 1920's consisted of a single folded sheet.

Not any more. Companies know that their share price is influenced not only by boring old results, but also by 'softer' factors—the strength of the Chairman's chin, the smile of the office receptionist, the overall 'feelgood' factor which an analyst gets on reading the report. In consequence, companies are prepared to put up large budgets to produce a document which will send a reassuring (if not realistic) message.

The emphasis on appearance inevitably means a de-emphasis on substance. Finance departments no longer run the show; that privilege goes to PR and Corporate Affairs departments, who are given free reign to polish up the company's image. The audience gets extended to customers, the press, the public at large , local authorities and Parliament. The report gets thicker, glossier, and more like a magazine. It sits in the lobby with the flowers.

There is nothing inherently wrong with this. Indeed, running the report and the corporate brochure together might be construed as an efficient use of shareholder's money. The problem arises when the words on the page appear to sabotage the company's intention to communicate. For instance:

> "The essentially speculative short-term asset playtype preference of local investors makes it difficult to invest directly in those companies which continue to show growth in the country's specialist areas of expertise."

As an instance of baffle-the-shareholder, this is an extreme example, but it does demonstrate the strangulated English in which many annual reports are written. Read enough of them, and you'll soon become familiar with the 'rationalised asset bases', the 'retrenchments to core businesses', and other elegant turns of phrase. The disease can even affect the way companies *think*. One MD recently wrote:

> "We're looking for bolt-on spin-offs"

Few companies set out to be deliberately vague or obscure in talking to their shareholders. Wording like this just tends to accrue in the process of putting the report together, and the people in overall charge sometimes lose their perspective on what is sesquipedalian and what isn't. There are two main reasons for this.

The first is a mistaken belief that readers will be impressed if the wording itself is weighty and sonorous. Too much of this sort of thing and the reader's brain becomes weary, and weary readers do not make enthusiastic shareholders.

The second and common trap lies in the way annual reports treat bad news. A study last year showed that the Chairmen of companies on the brink of collapse used longer words and sentences than Chairmen of more successful organisations. They resorted to the smoke-screen, hoping, perhaps, that a barrage of syllables would deflect attention from unpleasant reality. In fact any sensible reader is likely to think "what is this organisation hiding?"

As an investor, creditor or acquirer of a company, you need to be able to cut through all this flim-flam. Thumb quickly past the pages of grimacing employees presenting cheques to Cancer Research, ignore letters from the Chairman recounting how he skilfully guided the corporate ship through the twin reefs of recession and the foreign exchange crisis, and turn straight to the numbers in the back. What you want to know is whether they add up.

This concludes the basic course in accounting. (*Note*: this portion of the book is tax-deductible if you bought it to prepare for your PE2s)

ORGANISATIONAL BEHAVIOUR

THE STUDY OF ORGANISATIONAL behaviour goes all the way back to Machiavelli's *The Prince* — a chart-topper in the 15th century, and still the basic textbook today. But it didn't become a formal intellectual discipline until the Great Depression, when thousands of psychiatrists suddenly found their couches empty. Three pounds an hour was a lot of money in those days, and patients has more important things to do than take their emotions out for a jog.

Looking around, a few of these unemployed pioneers realised that the only depression victims still able to pay their fees weren't individuals at all; they were big, ailing companies. So it is that intellectual disciplines emerge.

O.B. is basically enhanced common sense. But to study it formally you must be able to speak the argot of its practitioners. After all, without jargon, there would be no need for experts. Get out the dictionary and memorise as many five-syllable words as possible. Then study the table on the next page and practise translating a few common-sense ideas into corresponding O.B.-speak.

They may sound strange at first, but you'll soon get the hang of these clumsy phrases. The trick is to learn which are current and which are passé. 'In' phrases at the moment are 'flexible culture', 'internal communication', and 'concensus'. 'Out' phrases are 'structure', 'hierarchy' and 'You're fired'.

Common-Sense Idea	Corresponding O.B. Jargon
Always say please and thank you.	Always practise mutuality of respect in conversational bookends.
Employee Darts match on Wednesday nights.	The Voluntary Association in Corporate Life : A Search for Meaning
When in Rome do as the Romans do	Observe the cultural norms and rituals of your host environment
Look before you leap	Develop a detailed action plan before commencing your implementation phase.

For some people, O.B. theory is just a conspiracy against plain English. Self-made businessmen who've come up the hard way tend to fret whenever the discussion turns to touchy-feely theoretical stuff—particularly when implementation of that theory is going to cost money. They *know* that production and sales *make* money for the company; every other department just wastes it.

Whilst a basic attitude of "does it contribute to the bottom line ?" is no bad thing, it is going too far to write off organisational theory as being of no practical value whatsoever. After all, properly organised, even crime pays.

The prudent course for high-fliers is to learn the basics of O.B. theory and no more. This applies whether you see yourself as a thrusting entrepreneur or a swift climber of corporate ladders

As an entrepreneur, you might be able to build your better mousetrap and raise the money to make and market it correctly, but unless you can make your employees do your bidding, you will be dead in the water. O.B. theory just might help you out.

As a corporate ladder-climber you will find that every company has at least one loon in a senior position who is into O.B. theory in a big way. Even if you think it *is* a load of tosh, keep it to yourself.

"You're the Internal Communications expert. You fire him."

Broadcasting your view may make you the company's leading expert in out-placement theory.

Sources of Motivation

The first thing to get a grip on in studying organisations is what makes people tick. Once you know the secret, you automatically have a wide range of *motivating levers* to use — with varying degree of subtlety — to make your subordinates hustle. O.B. theory recognises three main sources

of motivation :

(a) The need for achievement
(b) The need for power
(c) The need for affiliation

Not everyone agrees with this list. There are still a few die-hard companies who continue to rely on a primary motivator which has proved surprisingly durable over the centuries : the need for money.

Exactly which motivation lever you pull as a manager depends, ultimately, on your *own* sources of power. To be a successful manager you need five kinds of power, the most important of which are the power to *reward* and the power to *punish*. Commonly referred to as the carrot and the stick, these are relatively crude techniques according to modern organisational theory, but they can be strong motivators.

Examples of reward power would include a promotion, a salary increase, and a ticket to Centre Court on Men's Finals Day. Examples of punishment power would include a demotion, a transfer to the company's administration office in Romford, and a ticket to the over-35 Ladies Plate.

The other three types of executive power are more genteel : "Reverent" power is like hero worship — the kind of power which Mr Spock has over millions of 'Star Trek' fans. The man never actually existed in real life. He has no small talk. He hasn't even been on prime time television for ten years. Yet, the turnstiles humm at Trekkie conventions all over the world. No-one really knows what he does have that makes people submit to his will — some kind of charisma, aura, inner force . . . plus, of course, the pointy ears. 'Reverent power' seems as good a phrase as any.

'Legitimate' power is something entirely different. It stems not from the irresistible personality of the leader but from some kind of formal hierarchical relationship. You may think it's very unfair when your boss asks you to polish her BMW in your lunch hour, but you know that if you refuse, your next office will be one with no window, no desk, and a seat that flushes. You do it because her superior position in the hierarchy gives her legitimate power to make your life absolute hell.

Finally, there is 'expert' power — the respect accorded by the public to those they consider expert in a particular field. Expert power is commonly wielded by doctors (in medical matters), lawyers (in legal matters), accountants (in financial matters) and actors (sic) like Sting (in all matters pertaining to the environment and corporate responsibility).

The Three Styles of Management

One of the first things they teach you in O.B. theory is to think of every organisation as if it were a sovereign state, with its own language, customs, and history. Collectively, these are referred to as the organisation's internal culture.

Just as paleontologists divide the prehistoric era into Paleolithic and Neolithic periods, so organisational theorists recognise different types of internal culture. The current favourites are Theory X, Theory Y and Theory Z. (Theories A to W all had their day but have been generally scrapped as unworkable. They are still observable, however, in the French farm sector, the English cricket team, and the Iraqui military.)

Theory X reigned supreme from the start of the industrial revolution until the Second World War. The type of office it fostered would be unrecognisable to today's pampered pooches — no ergonomically-designed working 'pods', no subsidised canteen, no Nautilus gym rigs in the basement, — and often no *pay*. Just a no-frills sweat shop. The underlying assumption : given the choice between working and drinking coffee, most employees will drink coffee. Ipso facto, no Kenco.

Instead, you worked in an environment where the boss was the boss and you were mighty privileged to have a job.Theory X was long on 'legitimate' power systems, and short on the other four types. What it gave in productive output, it took in human cost.

It was supplanted in the post-War period by Theory Y, which works on the premise that, deep down, employees *like* working. They are only prevented from doing so by the arbitrary and authoritarian rules of society — like having to clock in every morning.

To get the most from a workforce, it was argued,the working culture has to be egalitarian and meritocratic. It has to be "an office without walls". Although this inevitably meant the loss of many privileges which managers had hitherto regarded as a virtual birthright — separate dining facilities, separate lavatories, being addressed as 'Mr' or 'Mrs' by anyone lower down the ladder— Theory Y became widely accepted as the model for internal office culture, and remains so today.

The UK's industrial relations record in the last three decades has, however, done little to validate the claims made on behalf of Theory Y. If the nation's workers are happier in their jobs, their contentment has certainly not fed through to improved economic performance.

Indeed, in the mid-1980's, executives began to look to the wise men of the East for new ideas on employee relations. They didn't have to look far, as the big Japanese car companies were already busy introducing their methods to new plants in Wales and Sunderland. Theory Z was right here on the doorstep.

Its starting point is that workers will show greater job commitment if the employer shows it "cares". The watchword is *loyalty* and it has to work both ways : in Japan employees are hired for life, and hardly ever sacked. If a highly-paid executive makes some huge strategic mistake, he is quietly exiled to the company cafeteria at his current salary where he spends the rest of his life serving soup in public humiliation.

In the UK, Theory Z is applied in watered-down form, and its most obvious manifestation is in the organisation of workers into 'quality circles'. Designed to foster a sense of corporate pride and unity of purpose, quality circles involve members of a production line or office getting together with management at the start of the day, and rapping out the company song together — risible, certainly, but at Nissan's plant, it seems to have worked. Body fitters, used to lining up panels to the nearest half-inch or so, have been working to near-Japanese standards of precision.

In general, however, British companies have been slow to take up the Theory Z mantle. This is in marked contrast to the *academics* specialising in Organisational Theory who are rooting hard for its success. Their enthusiasm could have something to do with the books they have written on the subject at £18.99 a throw. Or the fact that it is the last theory in the alphabet.

Like blood types, Theories X, Y and Z don't mix. On the following page, we provide a detailed guide to their essential differences.

There is one other trend in organisational theory worth watching — New Age spirituality. Management training groups have been pushing it very hard, holding conferences on 'Bringing Spirituality into the Organisation' and 'The Tao of Management'. Delegates so far include local authorities, charities and computer companies, but for most ordinary executives New Age-ism is still a little bit of a rarefied taste. It's gastronomic equivalent is sweetbread or tripe — undoubtedly good for you, but difficult to swallow.

Time will change this perception. New Age theory will shake off David Icke and the turquoise shellsuits, and gradually become absorbed into mainstream O.B. theory. On balance this is to be welcomed, if only because it's a lot more fun than Theory X.

Questions for Discussion

Perform a *cultural audit* of your own office or company. Does it conform to Theory X, Theory Y, or Theory Z? Or does it best exemplify Newton's Theory of Inertia ?

	SWEAT SHOP (1870-)	OFFICE WITHOUT WALLS (1970-)	BRAVE NEW OFFICE (1990-)
WORKING HOURS	*Theory X:* employees arrive at 6.45 A.M. 15 minutes before their boss, eat lunch at their desks, and head for home just after the boss leaves at 7.15 P.M.	*Theory Y:* Workers come and go according to their circadian rhythms. They don't see their boss for weeks on end; all communication is via pink "while you were out" pads.	*Theory Z:* Employees arrive at 8.00 A.M. for group calisthenics and singing of the company anthem. Lunch is eaten during one-hour quality conferences. Head for home at 5.02 P.M. ready for tomorrow's challenges.
TREATMENT OF SECRETARIES	*Theory X:* "Miss Johnson, type this letter and give me three clean carbons."	*Theory Y:* "Ms Johnson, I deliberately sidestepped difficult questions about your typing when I took you on last month, but would you consider getting this letter out for me by the end of the month ?"	*Theory Z:* "Katie-san, your superior typing performance this month brings much honour on our humble sales office. Take this letter as a token of my appreciation, and type it."
DELIVERING A LATE REPORT	*Theory X:* "Sir, here is the report you asked for. My apologies for its brevity, but it was difficult to include more than fifty pages of detail as I was only able to start at ten o'clock last night."	*Theory Y:* "Fred, got some rough notes on that report you wanted last week. Sorry about the delay, but I've been away on a three-day interpersonal skills workshops."	*Theory Z:* "Mitsuo-san, here's the report. Sorry it's late, but the company was counting on my backhand topspin to uphold our record against the Nissan Allstars this morning."

	SWEAT SHOP (1870-)	OFFICE WITHOUT WALLS (1970-)	BRAVE NEW OFFICE (1990-)
ASKING THE BOSS FOR A RISE	*Theory X*: "Sir, I've been with the firm ten years now and have begun to think of marriage. Do you think you might consider giving me a rise of a shilling a week, phased in over the next 18 months ?"	*Theory Y*: "Fred, my wife makes 20 per cent more than I do, *and* she gets free health care plus 6% pension contributions. Match it, or I walk."	*Theory Z*: "Mitsuo-san, I can no longer bear to live with the dishonour of making 15 per cent less than my counterparts at Volkswagen." (Draws hari-kari sword) "I would be most grateful if you would act as my second."
INCENTIVE SYSTEMS	*Theory X*: Meet your targets and you might be allowed to keep your job.	*Theory Y*: Come within spitting distance of your targets, and you don't have a thing to worry about.	*Theory Z*: Meet your targets, and you earn the undying respect and loyalty of your colleagues. Beat them by a mile, and you stand a chance of being made "Employee of the Week".
HOW EMPLOYEES ARE FIRED	*Theory X*: A yellow slip in Friday's pay envelope, with instructions to have your desk cleared out by lunchtime.	*Theory Y*: The employee is taken to lunch by the boss and asked to sign a letter waiving all rights against the company. He is then given free use of the photocopier and phone for 6 months to help him find another job — and himself.	*Theory Z*: They aren't

CORPORATE STRATEGY

CORPORATE STRATEGY IS for big picture types — those who, when watching an epic war film, identify with the High Command planning battle tactics on forty-foot table-tops, rather than the troops gutsing it out on the Front.

The military analogy suggests some of the great advantages of being a corporate strategist : comfort, security, and power. It suggests none of the disadvantages, because, unless you live for the adrenalin rush that comes with discomfort, insecurity and helplessness, there are none. Let's face it : would you rather plan a billion-pound acquisition from the splendour of corporate HQ or fight it out in the company trenches ?

What is corporate strategy, anyway ? Basically, it involves looking at your company's position in the marketplace and deciding on the best way to protect and enhance that position in the future.

The first thing you do is make an assessment of your company's *present* competitive strength. Are you caught in a squeeze between a market-dominating supplier and an equally monolithic customer ? Or do you have enough market power to demand lower prices from your suppliers and higher prices from customers ? Before you formulate a strategy, you need to know the answers. You may need to enquire even deeper — into the very *purpose* of your company's existence. It is not uncommon for managing directors to challenge their board with the deadly question "What business are we actually *in* ?" or (to use the increasingly prevalent American terminology) "What is our *mission* ?"

In these times of fickle consumer

behaviour and shifting world trade patterns, it is often not so easy to say what business you are actually in. It can be even more difficult to say what business you *should* be in, and recent history is replete with examples of disastrous corporate adventure into dangerous waters : Allied Lyons dropped a whopping £100 million in speculative Treasury operations in 1991; British and Commonwealth impaled itself on Atlantic Computers in 1990 and Ferranti danced its way over a cliff when it bought International Signal & Control. Even our own government was charmed into parting with £54 million of taxpayers' money by the silver-haired and silver-tongued John Zachary De Lorean.

For conglomerates trading in a number of different sectors the problem is particularly severe. Take GEC, whose £7 billion in sales dwarfs the gross national product of many countries in the United Nations. GEC makes everything from gas turbines to electrical switchgear to magnetic scanners to Hotpoint wash-dryers, and Lord Weinstock has a problem: how to keep track of his company's ten thousand different products. Which ones are profitable, which are growing, which require massive investment, and which should be unloaded pronto. In short, which businesses should GEC be in ?

When dealing with a company of this size, the consequence of one misjudged strategic decision can be catastrophic and long-lasting not just to shareholders but to the national economy. No managing director in his right mind wants to take responsibility for such unfortunate decisions. Fortunately, in this day and age, they rarely have to. Instead, for £100,000 a month and more, they call in the present-day industrial soothsayers — the 'strategy consultants' — thereby transferring culpability for any future disasters, while still collecting their six-figure salaries.*

Robert Townsend, in his classic book 'Up the Organisation', had this to say of strategy consultants:

> "The effective ones are the one-man shows. The institutional ones are disastrous. They waste time, cost money, demoralise and distract your best people, and don't solve problems. They are people who borrow your watch to tell you what time it is, and then walk off with it."

How on earth can strategy consultants take in the complexities of a huge organisation like GEC in a few short months, let alone make sensible recommendations for future strategy ? Answer: they rely on some-

---

*GEC is used here purely as an example of a large company.

THE GROWTH-SHARE MATRIX

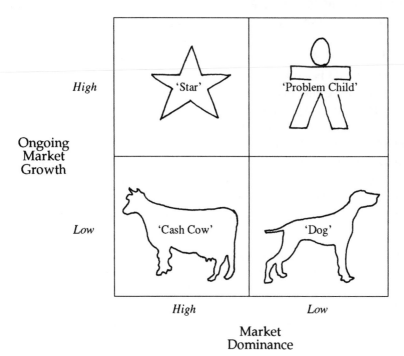

thing called a "growth/share matrix" to reduce complicated business activities into terms even a child could understand. These terms are: "Star", "Cash Cow", "Problem Child" and "Dog".

The first step is to assign to each different business one of the above terms. So what do they mean ?

1. Cash Cow

A cash cow is a product that dominates a mature no-growth industry, generating easy profits. The strategy is to milk it for everything it's worth, reinvesting profits in other products with better long-term growth prospects.

2. Star

A Star is a product dominating a fast-growing market. To maintain its position, you have to invest large amounts of money on a continuing basis — to build bigger plants, keep ahead of major technological advances, and so on. That way, you'll continue to reap rich harvests. Naturally, the source of this investment is your company's Cash Cow.

3. Problem Child

A Problem Child is a product competing, and losing out, in a growing market. There are two possible strategies for dealing with the Problem Child. If you're the risk-averse type, get rid of it and breathe a sigh of relief. If you're a gunslinger, invest heavily in the market's growth, hope that you can eventually raise your product's profile, and pray.

The trouble with problem children is that they are voracious consumers of cash, and never stop asking their parents for more. Sometimes, it's cruel to be kind.

4. Dog

A loser — the Problem Child who is thirty-three years old and never left home. The market is shrinking, and you are one of the unprofitable companies in it.

The suggested strategy : identify your Dogs while they are still Problem Children and sell them off before it's too late.

Why the obsession with market share ? Does it really matter or is it just a further example of the male preoccupation with size ? Well, in this instance, size does matter because, by and large, the more widgets you produce, the less they cost.

Imagine that the Rover and Citroen car groups each decided to launch a new contender in the executive car market. For each of them, it costs £250 million in research, design, engineering and factory costs just to get that first car off the production line. The second car might cost as little as £2,000. But whereas Citroen is part of the giant PSA group selling millions of cars a year worldwide, Rover is the lone survivor of the emasculated Leyland group selling only a fraction of that number. Citroen might sell three times as many of its model when all its European markets are taken into account, which means it can spread that initial £250 million three times more thinly. The same car that costs Rover £12,000 to bring to market might cost Citroen only £10,000. If consumers perceive that both models are equally good value, is it any wonder that Citroen makes a profit, while Rover struggles to break even?

In other words, if all else is equal, the largest company in an industry will have the lowest unit production costs and hence the highest potential profitability.

In many industries, all else is not equal. Take the market for *pens* of one kind or another. Patently, the

"Ah yes, Walker's pet project. Have a feasibility study done, and make sure it never sees the light of day."

companies in this market compete on factors other than cost : quality, durability, prestige, romantic association, and the ability to write upside down all come into it. Bic's strategy is to sell a basic biro in boxes of 50 for less than anyone else. They may make only .00666 pennies per biro, but as they shift more than a billion a year, they do alright out of it. Mont Blanc, on the other hand, cater for consumers who are willing to pay a thousand times more than the price of a Bic for a 'writing instrument' that looks nicer, and which they're proud to have in their breast pocket. Both Bic and Mont Blanc are profitable companies. The companies that *aren't* profitable are the ones caught in be-

tween : those trying to sell low-priced biros who can't sell as many as Bic — and who therefore have higher unit production costs — or those trying to sell expensive pens who can't command quite the same premium as Mont Blanc.

In most industries, therefore, this relationship between number of units sold and profitability looks something like a U-shaped curve. This is one of the fundamental canon's of corporate strategy.

To practise these techniques of analysis, read the following case study of an established American business and consider the best future strategy for the group.

THE
CORLEONE
FAMILY GROUP

INDUSTRY BACKGROUND

Businesses like the Corleone Family Group have their origins in the entrepreneurial culture of Mediterranean Europe. During the early years of the twentieth century, however, many of the small European operations set up subsidiaries in large cities across the USA. Several of them, including the Corleone Family Group, moved their operations across the Atlantic entirely. These companies experienced explosive growth between 1919 and 1934, during Prohibition. Key success factors included well-developed import-export operations, liquid cash reserves, and strict enforcement of contracts.

Following World War Two, however, the changing world economy brought an increasingly international character to the industry. Most firms opened trading bureaux in Istanbul, Marseilles and Bogota to streamline their distribution channels.

THE CORLEONE FAMILY GROUP

Organisation Chart in 1969

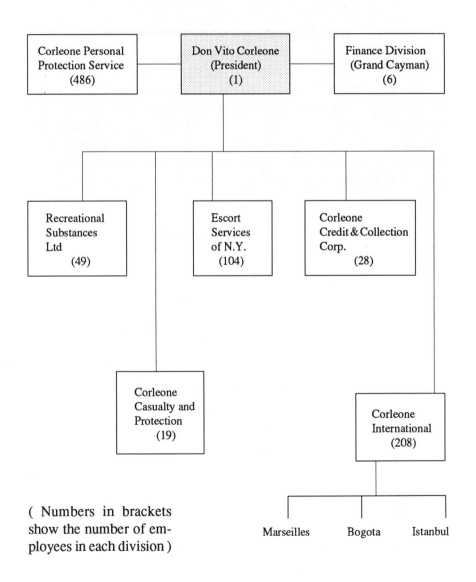

(Numbers in brackets show the number of employees in each division)

For many years the growth of the industry has been remarkably unconstrained by the necessity of paying taxes. Typical fixed costs include providing incentive compensation for key government officials in host countries, and employing a large number of highly-trained security guards to protect the firm and key management from involuntary liquidation.

THE 1969 CRISIS

By the late 1960s the Corleone Group was a highly diversified conglomerate, with annual turnover exceeding $90 million and profits of over $48 million. However, Don Vito Corleone, Head of the company, was becoming increasingly concerned about certain fundamental changes in some of the markets it served, and the impact they were having on his group.

Escort Services, for instance, one of the oldest divisions, was experiencing a deep decline in capacity utilisation because of growing free competition.

Recreational Substances Ltd, traditionally the largest division with over 95 per cent of the Greater New York market, was being subjected to intense competition from the rival Solozzo group. In the last year, the Solozzos had backward-integrated into poppy fields in Afganistan and were underpricing the Corleones by 30 per cent. The Don was wondering whether to adopt the classic solution of asking the president of the Solozzo group to take early retirement. Alternatively, perhaps the Corleones should backward-integrate as well. In recent months the Don had priced land in several locations in Asia, and had considered a hostile takeover of the Burpee Seed Corporation of Pennsylvania. The Don resolved to sound out the CEO of Burpee in the course of his next business meeting with Escort Services.

Finally, the Don was concerned about his firm's lack of management depth and long-term planning. Most members of his executive committee had experience only in narrow functional areas, like high-efficiency debt-collecting, Customs & Excise regulations, and labour relations. The Don felt a generalist's point of view was lacking.

Reluctantly, the Don placed a call to Miami, Florida.

THE CORLEONE FAMILY GROUP
Divisional Revenues in 1969
(in millions of dollars)

Division	Sales ($million)	Profit ($million)
Escort Services of New York	7.9	(2.5)
Recreational Substances Ltd	47.0	44.2
Corleone Credit and Collection Corp	4.7	4.5
Corleone Casualty and Collection	16.2	(2.3)
Corleone International	14.3	4.3
Total	**$90.1**	**$48.2**

THE MIAMI CONSULTING GROUP 1969 STUDY

MCG, a pioneer in the rapidly-growing field of "strategy consulting", was brought in by the Don to analyse the Corleone's long-range objectives. They spent six intensive months and billed $440,000 to perform an industry analysis and formulate a growth-share product portfolio for the Corleone group. In summary, the conclusions of the MCG study were as follows :

1. Escort Services : Losses of $2.5 million in 1969 on sales of $8 million. Capacity utilisation at an all-time low of 38 per cent. A fundamental, irreversible change in the marketplace has taken place, with product being made available at an unbeatable price : nothing. Recruitment is getting harder every year.

Recommendation : Pretty-page the financial statements, and sell to the expansion-minded Tattaglia family. This business is clearly a Dog.

2. Recreational Substances Ltd : Revenues in 1969 of $47 million with profits of $44 million (pre-tax and post-tax). Sales in traditional opium-derived product-lines are falling, though margins are still 95 per cent. The middle-class youth market for milder, pill-based products will continue to flower over the next ten years. Exploitation of this market will require considerable re-investment of profits in building up inventory, re-enforcing brand loyalty, and paying legal fees.

Recommendation : Use the cash thrown off from opium products to finance the tremendous growth in these youth lines. Let the retail network decline, through natural or if necessary natural-accelerated wastage, and concentrate on the defensible positions of importing and wholesaling. This business is clearly a Star.

3. Corleone Credit and Collection Corp : A small but profitable division. On loans oustanding of over $11 million, interest collected was $4.7 million, and profits $4.5 million. Multiple regression analysis indicates that the demand for CCCC loans is inversely proportionate to the health of the economy, and the division's competitive position in servicing the small-business sector is particularly strong when money supply is tight and usual loan sources dry up.

Recommendation : Keep this division small and nimble, as profitability in the banking industry clearly shows a U-shaped curve (see Figure 1). Milk it as a Cash Cow in the boom years, and continue current aggressive methods of receivables management. (Rapid

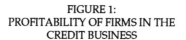

FIGURE 1:
PROFITABILITY OF FIRMS IN THE
CREDIT BUSINESS

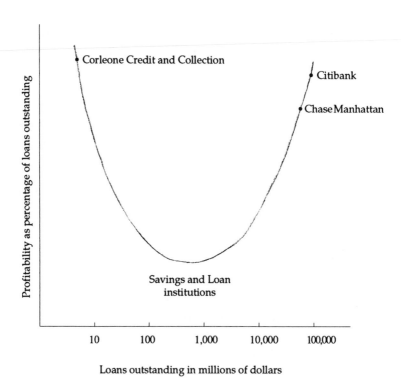

Loans outstanding in millions of dollars

foreclosure of overdue accounts by this division has, in the past, often led to the acquisition of valuable new businesses by the Corleone Family Group.)

4. Corleone Casualty & Protection : A real Problem Child, this division was acquired last year from the estate of its late president, Sal Teneglia. It has only a 3 per cent market share, and totally lacks credibility among its potential customers because the market is dominated by the Barzini group, which holds the other 97 per cent. The Barzinis are likely to resist any further erosion of their market share by use of unfair competition practices.

Recommendation : Divest this division to the highest bidder — probably the Barzini family. Tomorrow would be soon enough.

THE CURRENT CRISIS

"Eh, Michael . . . . so what we gonna do ?"

The man speaking is Don Vito Corleone. It is 1976. His hair is a distinguished gray, his body hard, over-sized. He is speaking to his youngest son, Michael, a recent graduate from business school.

"Papa, I just don't know. I think we need to bring back that big-gun consulting firm." He looked at his watch : midnight. "Some of my classmates are probably still in the office, I could give them a call right now."

The elder Corleone thought for a moment. Looking back, he realised that MCG's 1969 recommendations had been of enormous value. In the six years since the study, Corleone revenues had grown to nearly $267 million. He had sold Casualty & Protection Corp and Escort Services, and focused resources on the increasingly successful import/export operations. Profits were at an all-time high and Michael Corleone had taken over as executive Vice-President. But just recently the New Jersey State Legislature had passed a bill legalising gambling in Atlantic City. Who could guess what impact that would have on the Corleone family business ?

Other regional firms from Nevada, Chicago, and Providence were sending representatives to Atlantic City to assemble prime boardwalk real estate. The Don wondered whether he should continue focusing on current activities or risk entering what was shaping up as an all-out competitive war for market-share in the East Coast legalised gambling industry.

As he picked up the phone to request the advice of MCG in

evaluating his current strategic alternatives, the Don hesitated for a moment, remembering the six-figure fee which their last study had cost him. Putting the phone back on its cradle, the thought crossed his mind that now was the time to divesify into the most profitable racket of all : strategy consulting.

Questions for Discussion

• What overall strategy would you have recommended for the Corleone Family Group in the 1976 crisis ?

• Should the Don have gambled on entering the Atlantic City market ?

•Summarise the types of competitive weapons that help a company dominate in this industry.

PACKAGING YOURSELF

CHOOSING A CAREER

YOU HAVE JUST COMPLETED the basic course work to become a high-flier. Now it is time to start thinking about which area of business you want to be in. Just because you are already *in* a business doesn't mean you shouldn't re-assess your position in the light of where you'd *rather* be — unless you've given up hope for a better life altogether.

Different areas of business have varying degrees of tangible output. *Production* is concerned with producing an appliance or car efficiently.

"I have a daughter who teaches and a son who's a civil engineer. Sometimes I wonder where we went wrong."

Look, alfaalfa hyprodronics is going to be *the* growth business of the next decade, no doubt about it. All I need is five million seed capital to get it off the ground.

Sounds like the sort of area some of my clients might like to get into. I'll certainly make enquiries, if you like. By the way our fee scale starts at 7 per cent and climbs to . . . .

Do you know, the average 5 year-old only plays two hours of computer games per week ? I said to Nintendo, we could devise a campaign that would double that figure in three months.

Is that right ? I once audited a software company, and never saw such sloppy financial control in my life. I don't think they'd even heard of asset-amortisation . .

Well, I don't know about computers, but in household bleaches, on-pack coupons work best. This wholesaler told me last week he shifted two pallets as soon as they went on promotion !

The Entrepreneur
Talks a good game, but is actually scrounging for next meal. Wears a £400 Armani suit, bought three years ago when he felt flush. Motto : "Think big"

The Merchant Banker
Shell-shocked by recession. Still waiting for first big deal of the 90's. Has two-year old son he's never seen. Motto : "Thank God it's Friday. Only two more working days til Monday."

The Advertising Executive
Went into advertising for the sybaritic West End lifestyle and found herself shunted out to the E1 Dead Zone. Motto: "There's no promotion like self-promotion."

The Accountant
Hates small talk. Would have become an actuary if he'd had more personality. Four more years of slogging and he's up for partnership. Motto: "Better safe than sorry."

The Sales Manager
Once had his sights on doing a 'Paul Judge' MBO.Now glad just to keep his Scorpio.Drinks whatever his customers drink, only more. Motto: "Go for it."

When I joined JCB fifteen years ago, no-one had heard of *just-in-time*. Now the average stock time on the 3CX Backloader is 4.2% better than any of our competitors.

Yes, but what about labour rates? In South Korea, our workforce is not only skilled and dedicated. The average monthly wage is 70% less than in the West. Just one bowl—

In the long term, that can't work. Employers have to to *earn* loyalty by providing good pay, health care, creches and counselling. Take our Quality Programme, for instance . . .

Look: if Short restricts both white Bishops — Be4 16c5 Be7 17Bd3! Kasparov *is* vulnerable. He has to play Kxg7, Qxh6 29. Short wins !

Interesting. I don't play myself, but I've often thought that here at McKinsey's we are the sort of 'Grandmasters', of the business world.

The Production Engineer
Company tie, wears hard hat as protection from the paper-pushers above him. Motto: "Get it out the door."

Taiwanese Minister of Trade
Met English wife while studying engineering at Imperial. Spends eight months of the year touring Western plants to stay 'current' with latest technology. Motto: "Export or die."

The Personnel Manager
Graduated in Sociology at Kent University, before switching to something employable. Motto: 'People, not profits."

The Information Technology Specialist
Mad staring eyes. Blinks only once every four minutes. Makes money on the side running computer-dating agency. Motto: "Garbage in, garbage out."

The Strategy Consultant
Peripatetic existence. Embarrassed by displays of human affection, though not by obscene fees. Motto: "Have spreadsheet, will travel."

Sales and marketing get the product to the customer. The output in each case is obvious. *Personnel departments*, on the other hand, have an output that is less tangible — unless you're prepared to give some quantitative measure to office circulars of the "All employees *must* notify Personnel of their holiday dates for 1995 by 5th July 93" variety. Finally, there is *Finance*, which has almost no concrete output whatsoever.

The different areas of business activity are illustrated on the scale below. Most high-fliers choose a career towards the bottom of what is known as the "Line of Direct Labour." This is because they know that salary levels are inextricably linked with levels of measurable output.

Thus, an exceptional industrialist, responsible for a company which produces two million washing machines a year, gets £75,000 max. A successful insolvency lawyer, who wanders corporate battlefields firing bullets of mercy into the heads of debt-laden conglomerates, is good for a couple of hundred.

CONCRETE OUTPUT

Assembly-line Worker	£12,000
Production Manager	£16,000
R&D	£18,000
Sales	£25,000
Advertising	£45,000
Finance	£80,000
Strategic Consulting	£120,000
Lawyer	£175,000

ABSTRACT OUTPUT

C.V. EXPANSION

IT'S AN UNFORTUNATE TRUTH that most personnel officers are so short of imagination and critical ability, that the first hurdle any C.V. has to leap is a presentational rather than a substantive one : if you set down your qualifications for the job using a 1947 Smith-Corona, not even straight A grades will save you. Smart embossed paper, top-of-the-range paper clips, and a sophisticated word-processed layout is now de rigeur just to get off the chocks.

In this respect, CVs conform to that old adage about success in politics : popularity is determined 80% by appearance, 20% by substance.

As it has become progressively more difficult to land jobs, DTP outfits have cottoned on to the effort which candidates are prepared to put into their CVs, and the small ads are now stuffed with offers to produce 'the perfect CV' for you. If you don't fancy spending £50 with them, take your pick from any number of guides available in bookshops.

The effect of all these CV-improvement schemes is that the minimum standard of appearance for acceptable CVs is now about the same as an average issue of Vogue.

What the guides forget to tell you, and what you should remember, is that whilst a polished appearance is essential, it isn't *sufficient.* Too many candidates imagine that, because they've packaged their credentials in some very pretty underwear, it can't fail to turn on its examiner. In fact, the job market is blessed and cursed by a surfeit of pretty underwear, and examiners can afford to be choosy. What they look for, ultimately, lies on the inside.

The implications are clear : if your CV doesn't already contain the sort of credentials which employers swoon over, start working on it. A well-crafted CV will transform the insipid into the inspired, the mundane into the magnificent, and the

"Two years pumping up tyres on a garage forecourt . . .hmmm . . . Why don't we change that to 'Experienced Airline Executive'."

illegal into the entrepreneurial. A straight-shooting CV will not. If you want to tell the unvarnished truth, that is your prerogative. So is unemployment.

This is not to imply that you should lie — only that you should describe your achievements in terms that give them dignity and prestige, a process known as CV *expansion*. Supposing you once had a summer job mowing lawns at your local cemetery. Hardly going to have employers chasing their tails, is it ? Not phrased like that, anyway. But think again. How else could that experience be described ? What about "Environmental officer with *500 men*

under me" ? See ? It's just a question of approaching the problem laterally.

The most important thing here is patience : if you stop writing when your CV reads merely as that of a credible contender, you might as well pack up and go home. Instead, even when applying for a graduate-entry job, keep honing the text until you look like a good candidate for next Secretary-General of the World Bank.

With this commitment to excellence in mind, the writing itself is simple. Begin with a blank pad of paper and list everything you have done since school, no matter how insignificant. Don't worry if your list looks a bit dull. It ought to be — business itself can be dull. Don't worry if some of the things you've written down seem trivial. Sometimes the most trivial achievements can be expanded the best. Remember, without CV expansion, *no-one* would ever get a job.

When you have finished your list, you are ready to begin the creative stage. Using the collection of *action* words at the end of this chapter, upgrade your list, word-by-word, so that it includes at least twenty of these words, consecutively if possible. The final product should look like a CV Ernie Harrison would envy.

If it doesn't . . . . . upgrade again.

Andrew Sinclair was a job applicant who used this technique. Born into an ordinary middle-class family in Preston, Lancashire, he had an academically successful but otherwise unremarkable three years at Leeds University. On the face of it, it looked like his lack of work experience would doom him to a decade of penal servitude on some dead-end graduate traineeship. Instead, by careful application of the principles just expounded, Andrew was able to turn his meagre summer job into a corporate recruiter's dream. Notice how his CV evolves from a scribbled work-sheet to a finished product.

Curriculum Vitae
ANDREW SINCLAIR

Education

1. School : Scarsdale Comprehensive, Preston.
   — 'A'-level project researching 0898-numbers, + social issues thereof.
2. University : Brunel, reading Economics
   — degree expected in June (God willing!)
   — bailed out a couple of times for my tutor when he & spouse in London.
   — dealt a little in hash to keep me in funds when the old man cut me off.

Work Experience

1. <u>June 1989: Greenview Country Club (Caddy)</u>
   — found golfers' balls
   — replaced divots
   — tended the pin
   — arranged players' betting pools.
   — stepped on opponents' balls in the rough.

2. <u>June 1990: Kentucky Fried Chicken (Cook)</u>
   — Biggest one in Leeds.
   — Cooked approx. 400 pieces-a-night.
   — took home extra chicken if I cooked too much
   — taught junior trainees sales techniques eg. "...and would you like a drink with your meal sir?" (always go for the extra sale..)

<u>Other</u> 1991: won £7,500 in McDonald's "Build a Big Mac" competition.
   — spent winnings on W-reg Jaguar XJS
   — Wrote off XJS crashing into local nightclub driving home blotto from party.
   — Sold remains of car to pay damages to nightclub boss.

Curriculum Vitae : Andrew Sinclair

Career Objective
A position offering challenge,
personal growth and serious *dineros*

Education

1990-1991   •A level Business Studies project: *'Telemarketing: an Analysis of Current Best Practice'*.

1987-1990   **West of England University (formerly Frome Poly)**
•Honours Economics Degree, Class 2 (viva)
•Established primary day-care facility for faculty children.
•Paid for tuition and living expenses in last two years by founding a small business marketing a complete line of leisure products to students, achieving return on investment of 2,013 per cent.
•Final Year Thesis : *'David Bowie : The Last Existential Man'*

Work Experience

Summer 1989   **Golf Co-ordinator : Greenview Country Club**
•Responsible for revitalisation of golf course to achieve improved playing characteristics.
•Provided financial consultancy service to members.
•Helped ensure members' strategic success by repositioning them vis-a-vis competitors.

Summer 1990   **Special Assistant to Franchisor, Kentucky Fried Chicken.**
•Senior production officer during high-volume evening shift.
• Audited inventory stocking levels and instituted control systems to prevent exceeding storage capacity. Conducted initial employee training and implemented employee motivation seminars.

Other Achievements

•Financed living expenses by winning £10,000 special construction project from national restaurant chain. (Was forced to dispose of major asset, however, after confrontation with obstructive local interests)

FIFTY SUGGESTED
ACTION VERBS
(A partial list)

Accumulated	Insisted
Achieved	Instituted
Acquired	Introduced
Audited	Leveraged
Awarded	Managed
Balanced	Manoeuvred
Collaborated	Monitored
Considered	Multiplied
Consulted	Obtained
Deduced	Packaged
Deployed	Produced
Designed	Profited
Determined	Promoted
Disposed	Quadrupled
Divested	Realised
Doubled	Repositioned
Enhanced	Resolved
Established	Rewarded
Finessed	Revitalised
Formulated	Selected
Founded	Served
Improved	Specified
Inaugurated	Succeeded
Inflated	Tripled
Initiated	Triumphed

INTERVIEWING STRATEGY

AFTER YOUR EXPANDED CV has catapulted you across the front lines of a company, brace yourself for eyeball to eyeball confrontation in that deadliest of all business rituals — the job interview.

On rare occasions, interviews can actually be fun — when, for instance, a top-level headhunter is trying to lure you away from a pleasant-enough £60,000 job into a pleasanter-still £80,000 one. But for the rest of us, and certainly for rookie graduates, nothing makes your ticker beat quite so fast as an impending run-in with a potential employer.

Sending out your CV, after all, is like firing endless long-range salvos into the night : if some distant executive doesn't believe your claims of earning £100,000 from a campus pizza-delivery operation, he can simply toss your CV into the bin. That's a lot easier to take than watching a senior executive in a pin-stripe suit laugh in your face at point-blank range.

But the clammy palms and elevated blood pressure we all face *can* be minimised — and your chances of being taken on maximised — if you develop a custom-tailored interviewing strategy appropriate for each interview.

Strategy Formulation

Imagine you are an overworked recruitment director in one of the few companies still active on the university milk round. Your brief is to sign up three bright undergraduates to start next September. Plucked from your comfortable carpeted office,

"Mr Stephens, if I had any qualms about churning, I would hardly be applying for a job in a butter factory."

you are holed up for a whole week in the sort of provincial hotel that thinks the height of luxury is equipping each room with a kettle and three sachets of instant coffee. Day after day you trudge into campus to meet a parade of the most painfully eager faces you've ever seen. Eighty similar CVs expanded beyond recognition; eighty similar life stories. How can you possibly choose ?

Seasoned interviewers know the answer: you screen the CVs on the train and make your three selections in advance. If these three do not come across in person as total morons, they're in. The only chance for the other seventy-seven is if one of the first three blows it.

This is where strategy comes in. The night before you have an interview, think about how well your qualifications fit you for the job in question, and put yourself into one of the following categories :

(a) I *should* get this job.
(b) I *might* get this job, with luck.
(c) It would be a *travesty* if I got this job.

Corresponding to each category is a distinct interviewing strategy. The following example assumes that three different candidates are going for the same banking job. See the different approaches they take.

Category 1: "I *should* get this job"

Candidate 1 has the ideal background: educated at a public school known for producing solid intellectuals as opposed to rah-rah Lloyds underwriters, or (better still) at a top-notch state school, he has just graduated with a double-first in economics & law from Oxford or Cambridge. As an undergraduate he held at least one of the following posts and, preferably, all three at the same time : President of the Union, Editor of Isis/Producer of Footlights, Full Blue.

During consecutive summer holidays he has built up a minimum of 6 months experience in a relevant industry, and has had two articles in trade magazines acclaimed for their 'novel outlook' or 'fresh insights.'

Proper Interview Strategy : the Confident Approach

The candidate expects to be chosen and can afford to let the interviewer draw out the relevant facts, as they are written on his CV anyway. He should appear enthusiastic but understated. His clothing must be elegant and utterly conservative. If he doesn't lose consciousness during the interview, it's in the bag.

Category 2: "I *might* get this job, with luck"

Candidate 2 has a very strong record, but one that is not *quite* right for this job. He got a good 2:1 at Bristol, Exeter or Durham, but in philosophy rather than economics. He wins points for being Treasurer of the university's Stock Exchange Society but immediately loses them again for founding the Society of Teddy Bear Lovers. He has spent some of his holidays working in relevant industries, but has also had jobs of less obvious relevance, notably a whole summer shovelling stable strudel in his local riding school.

Proper Interviewing Strategy: The Hard-Charging Approach.

Candidate 2 has to be pro-active in guiding the conversation where he wants it to go. He has to pitch straight into his main achievements, keep talking about them unless and until the interviewer's eyes close, and take prompt action if it looks at any time as if the discussion is going to drift onto the less impressive aspects of his career.

The danger of this mandate is that he may appear egotistical or evasive. That doesn't really matter. Egotism and evasiveness are advantages in many businesses. As long as he doesn't come over as aggressive, he has a chance of getting the job.

Category 3: "'It would be a travesty if I got this job"

Candidate 3 is as well qualified as the other candidates from a professional standpoint, but has virtually no chance of getting the job because of her unacceptably eclectic background. She graduated ten years ago with a double-first from Buckingham University, helped organise the Reading Rock Festival for three years on the trot, then underwent deprogramming to become a disciple of the Reverend Moon. She was rapidly promoted to Portfolio Manager of the organisation's UK property holdings, but fell out with her mentor over tenant removal policies and enrolled for an MBA. Unfortunately she neglected her studies to capitalise on the foreign exchange crisis of 1992, and was unable to take her final MBA papers.

Proper Interviewing Strategy : The High-Rolling Approach

Candidate 3 hasn't got a chance of getting the job unless she adopts an unconventional strategy. Her only hope is to go as off-the-wall as pos-

GROOMING YOURSELF FOR INTERVIEW

One of the more difficult areas on which to make recommendations, because there's a limit to what you can do if your face doesn't fit. You may be the best business brain of your year, but if you deport yourself like Mr Bean's idiot sibling, not even a reference from Lord Hanson will get you in.

Neverthless, there are various elements of appearance and posture that you should be aiming for. With work and a bit of practice, you can get surprisingly good results from even the most unpromising physical material.

1. Eyes

Must be purposeful and thoughtful, with just the right number of blinks per minute. If you blink too often, you'll come over as a bit of an oddball and be deemed unpresentable to the company's clients; if too seldom, you'll remind them of Attenborough in '10 Rillington Place' — an even less acceptable proposition.

2. Mouth

Short of dribbling onto your tie or leering like Rik Mayall, you should be alright with whatever kisser God gave you. If you plan to be a financial adviser, however, add a hint of ruthlessness to your appearance by occasionally pursing your lips in a cruel thin smile. You don't want the interviewer to doubt your resolve when it comes to gambling pensioners' savings on the cocoa market.

3. Expression

Decisive, authoritative, cynical, manipulative, calculating, are some of the descriptions to go for. A tall order for one face, granted, especially while tackling Eyes and Mouth at the same time, so take it slowly. Start with a couple at a time, and work your way up.

sible and hope she lucks into an interviewer who finds her candour and originality refreshing.

Warning : the high-rolling approach never works if the selection process involves more than one interview.

Preparing your Mind : A Pre-flight Checkout

You've spent years building up your CV and interpersonal skills for this moment. You *know* that you have to be incisive, perceptive, and articulate. You *know* that in business, self-confidence and control are everything. You *know* that if you come across as gushing or impressionable, you've blown it. And you *know* that ten minutes before you're called in to the interview room your bowels will liquify, your brain will go AWOL, and your normal grace and poise will mysteriously disappear.

It doesn't have to be like this. With practice, anyone can get a handle on interviewing technique. Imagine that you aren't going to be **interviewed** as such, but that you are boarding an aeroplane to give the interviewer a brief aerial tour of your past. With that concept in mind, we'll follow our three candidates in their

search for a typical corporate finance job :

Morgan Grenfell
Finsbury Square
Boardroom 17 4.30 pm

Phase One: Boarding

The **confident candidate** arrives precisely one minute before the appointed time. He wears a black single-breasted suit from Hackett — with lapels that are, by instinct, exactly the same width as those of his interviewer — a Thomas Pink double-cuffed shirt, and a red silk tie. When invited in by the interviewer, he gives a firm handshake and says, "Good afternoon Mr Wallace, I am ... "

The **hard-charging candidate** arrives half-an-hour before his appointment and spends the time pacing around the reception area, glancing through the reception copy of the FT, and making trips to the lavatory. He wears a suit from The Suit Co., Italian brogues, and a button-down shirt from Blazer. As soon as the door to the interview room opens, he lunges forward, wrenches the interviewer's hand in a crushing handshake, and declares "Mr

Wallace, delighted to meet you . . ."

The **high-rolling candidate** wears her most comfortable pair of jeans, a Merino polo neck, and Nike trainers — not going out of her way to impress anybody. As the interviewer opens the door, she folds her copy of NME under her arm, shakes his hand, assumes the lotus position, and says, "I'm Jane Raikes, remember — the ex-Moonie ?"

Phase Two: Taxiing

The interviewer and candidate take their seats. The interviewer reaches for a jug of filter coffee sitting on a hot-plate and says "In our job, this stuff keeps us going. Like some ?"

Confident: "Freshly-ground Arabica, if I'm not mistaken . . . and I'm not. How very civilised, I'd love a cup."

Hard Charger: "Well, I try to make a point of having only one cup for every two hours solid work, and I've already had four today, but . . . yes, I'd like one, thankyou."

High-Roller: "Do you *know* how much native bean-pickers get paid ? You should buy Brazilocaf. All the profits are ploughed straight back into indigenous enterprise schemes. Okay, so it tastes like the splashback of a Sao Paulo latrine in the guava season, but . . ."

Phase Three: Taking Off

The interviewer pursues his first line of serious questioning, looking for depth and a reasoned response from the candidates: "So, what talents do you think you would bring to Morgan Grenfell?"

Confident: "To be honest, I think my strongest asset is my ability to get along well with people. In addition, my degree gave me a good foundation in economic theory, and Acquisitions Monthly have just published my paper on East European project finance — it's on my CV but I'd be happy to amplify if you want."

Hard-Charger: "I'm hungry and aggressive and have always excelled in everything I've put my mind to. Frankly, I think that within two years of getting my feet under the desk, I could be the number one fee-earner in the department."

High-Roller: "I've got the Midas touch. I got out of equities in September '87 and made a killing on Forex in August this year. (Sits back and lights a cigarette) Let's face it: most of the people you'll be seeing have never managed an asset more valuable than their Golf GTi."

Cruising at Altitude

The interviewer now asks a loaded question designed to draw out the candidate's political views. "Tell me, what did you think of the government's decision to suspend membership of the ERM ? "

Confident: "Time will tell whether it was right or not, but I think you're being generous calling it a *decision*" (They both laugh.)

Hard-Charger: "In my last term at Bristol, I demolished the Cambridge Debating Team with a speech on just that subject. And the answer, unequivocally, is no."

High-Roller: "Fantastic for me . . . and George Soros."

Phase Five : Circling

The interviewer checks his watch: three minutes to go. He winds down the conversation. "Well, anything you'd like to ask me before we finish ?"

Confident: "I think I should mention that I've been invited to present a paper to Harvard in mid-October. I assume that it would be acceptable if I arranged my work schedule around that visit."

Hard Charger: "Yes. I wondered how much of your work is for international clients. I haven't had a chance to mention it, but I'm fluent in Spanish and Arabic and I'd like to brush up on my Japanese."

High Roller: "I was wondering if you have ever considered becoming a distributor for NSA water filters ? I made over £25,000 last year with a network built up in my spare time. (Produces a brochure) If you're interested I'll arrange a demonstration."

Phase Six : Landing

The interviewer stands up, and extends his hand. "It's been very nice meeting you. We'll be in touch, and have a good journey home "

Confident: "Thank you. I've

enjoyed it too. See you in September." He smiles.

Hard Charger: "Thank you. By the way, I've got several other highly competitive offers on hold, so if you could get back to me by the end of the week, I'd appreciate it."

High Roller: "So, what do you think ? Have I got the job ?" If the answer is negative, or if the interviewer starts talking about a second interview, the candidate shakes the interviewer's hand and gives him a jolt of her joy buzzer.

How to Decide which Approach Suits You

Deciding whether you should adopt a confident, hard-charging or high-rolling approach requires a careful assessment of how well your CV appears to fit the job. Try to look at it from the interviewer's point of view, and the correct approach will suggest itself.

However, you may occasionally find yourself applying for positions outside your realm of experience — in other words, where you haven't a clue what the job's about but the salary looks interesting. In these situations, don't ring up the recruitment department, declare your interest, and then ask what is it that a Convertible Swaps Analyst actually does. What you must do is send in your CV anyway, and analyse the letter you get in reply. By carefully reading between the lines, you will be able to determine what initial judgements the company has made about you, and what approach you should adopt in interview.

By way of illustration, you will find on the following pages three standard replies which have been sent to Andrew Sinclair, and our translations showing what the company *really* meant in each case.

Example 1: an encouraging letter suggesting adoption of the hard-charging approach

WHAT THE COMPANY *SAID* :

VAIN & COMPANY

STRATEGY CONSULTANTS
ONE PIE AVENUE · LONDON · EC3A 4HZ

Mr Andrew Sinclair
42 Albermarle Road
York
YO1 1EP

May 9th 1993

Dear Mr Sinclair

Thank you for your recent enquiry about working for Vain & Company. The Recruitment Committee has reviewed your curriculum vitae, and we are impressed with your qualifications.

We intend to recruit five graduate trainees for the coming September, and would like to invite you for interview at our offices at 11 am on Monday 27th June. Please call my secretary, Jasmine, to confirm this appointment or, if the scheduled time is not convenient, to arrange an alternative appointment.

Thank you for your interest in Vain & Company, and I look forward to meeting you next month.

Yours sincerely,

Thomas Drake
Recruitment Partner

LONDON   PARIS   FRANKFURT   NEW YORK   BOSTON   TOKYO   MADRID

WHAT THE COMPANY *MEANT:*

VAIN & COMPANY

MANAGEMENT CONSULTANTS
ONE PIE AVENUE • LONDON • EC3A 4HZ

Mr Andrew Sinclair
42 Albermarle Road
York
YO1 1EP   May 9th 1993

Dear Mr Sinclair

Thanks for the letter and CV. I have to admit I was impressed: your ability to get words like "strategic success" and "implemented" into an otherwise unremarkable CV suggest that you're just the sort of jargon-junkie we need in the glamour world of strategic consulting. I'm quite a bullshitter myself, but it's still good to listen to an expert.

Vain & Company has averaged 30% growth a year for the last decade. Our recruitment strategy is based on creaming off the best graduates from the top universities before our corporate clients get them. That way we can bill you out for ten times what they'd have to pay you as an employee.

Whether you possess the appearance and style it takes to convince a 60 year-old M.D. that he needs a 23 year-old greenhorn to help him run his company is another matter. You'd better come down, and we'll put you through your paces.

Yours sincerely,
Thomas Drake
Recruitment Partner

LONDON   PARIS   FRANKFURT   NEW YORK   BOSTON   TOKYO   MADRID

Example 2 : an unencouraging letter suggesting adoption of the high-rolling approach

WHAT THE COMPANY *SAID* :

RED SPARROW FILM PRODUCTIONS

THE OLD ABBATTOIR
CUTLER'S WHARF
MANCHESTER M2 4LB

Mr Andrew Sinclair
42 Albemarle Road
York
YO1 1EP   9/5/93

Dear Andrew

Thank you for your letter asking about vacancies as a production
assistant.

We are a young company in a competitive business, and only take
on staff if they are exceptionally well-qualified. On the face
of it, you lack key experience in our field, but if you think
you have something very special to offer and are passing this
way, I'd be happy to hear what you have to say.

Regards

Jessy Scales

WHAT THE COMPANY *MEANT:*

RED SPARROW FILM PRODUCTIONS

**THE OLD ABBATTOIR
CUTLER'S WHARF
MANCHESTER M2 4LB**

Mr Andrew Sinclair
42 Albermarle Road
York
YO1 1EP   9/5/93

Dear Andrew

Since they wrote us up in GQ last month, I've been getting hundreds
of letters a week from you over-educated public schoolboys. I've been
in this business for 15 years and I've never met anyone with more
than one O-level who had the backbone to make it.

The reality is that the film business is about as glamorous as
sweeping Earls Court after the Horse of the Year Show. And it pays
about the same. Take my advice and get into banking.

I suppose it's just possible that you have some huge trust fund to
dip into, or that you're Michael Grade's godson. If so, feel free
to drop in and we can talk turkey.

Regards,

Jessy Scales

Example 3 :the blatant rejection letter (a.k.a. "The Bullet")

WHAT THE COMPANY *SAID :*

CROESUS PARTNERS
Vulture Capital
PO Box 932, Bristol BS4

Mr Andrew Sinclair
42 Albermarle Road
York
YO1 1EP   May 9th 1993

Dear Mr Sinclair

Thank you for sending me your letter and CV regarding a position with us.

As you may be aware, we very seldom take on graduates, and this year we have received an enormous number of applications. Inevitably, we cannot see as many candidates as we would like to, and we have to make difficult decisions on extremely limited information with respect to the suitability of each candidate.

Whilst we were impressed with your credentials we unfortunately will not be able to invite you for interview on this occasion. We will, however, keep your details on file, and consider you should any vacancies arise in the future.

Thank you for your interest in Croesus Partners, and we wish you luck in your career.

Yours sincerely,

Godfrey Hammerhead
Managing Partner

WHAT THE COMPANY *MEANT:*

CROESUS PARTNERS
Vulture Capital
PO Box 932, Bristol BS4 0PQ

Mr Andrew Sinclair
42 Albermarle Road
York
YO1 1EP   May 9th 1993

Dear Mr Sinclair

My compliments — that CV looks pretty sharp: the bold type, the boxed-off sections, the embossed paper, even stamping the envelope <u>confidential </u>to distinguish it from the rest of our junk mail. You blokes know all the tricks.

Our business is about backing winners to the hilt and showing losers the door. To be frank, I fail to see how being a reconstructed fast-food flunkie qualifies you to make those sorts of judgements — unless there's more to serving up Two Pieces with Regular Fries than meets the eye.

That said, I've learned over the years that it's not worth insulting lightweights who have the temerity to ask for a job. Today's reject just might end up as head of Glaxo, or oppose us in a leveraged buy-out through pure spite. Hopefully, this personalised letter dashed off on Word 5 will keep you sweet.

Yours sincerely,

Godfrey Hammerhead
<u>Managing Partner</u>

How to Answer the Ten Most Loaded Interviewing Questions of All Time : A Self-Teaching Quiz

1. Why did you do a degree in fine arts instead of something more practical ..... like accountancy ?
(a) I knew I was destined for a business career even then, but felt — and still feel — that it is important to be a well-rounded individual.
(b) (Sobbing:) I was young, foolish, . . . easily misled.
(c) The social life was much better in fine arts.
(d) I wanted to get in on the coming boom in pre-Colombian art.

2. Why did you leave your last job ?
(a) They couldn't keep me busy beyong 8 or 9 in the evening — and I just hate working with part-timers.
(b) The Managing Director's wife became pregnant. He didn't appreciate my circular denying responsibility.
(c) I'd been there 8 months and felt it was time to try something different.

3. Why do you want to join a big company like ours ?
(a) To lead the re-industrialisation of Britain.
(b) My uncle says you're a pretty good outfit .... and he should know — he's your biggest customer.
(c) I've got an aptitude for business — even my Probation Officer thinks so.
(d) Your holiday and pensions policy is legendary.

4. Did you read the article about Wheeler-Frye's new brand accounting policy in the FT ?
(a) Didn't everybody ?
(b) Yes, but the real story was in April's *Accountancy Age.*
(c) No. I've always thought the business coverage was better in The Mirror.
(d) Wheeler-Frye. Aren't they the back-up band for Fleetwood Mac ?

5. How would you feel about starting off at our distribution depot in Milton Keynes ?

(a) Whatever's best for the company.

(b) Great ! I just love American-style grid cities !

(c) To be honest, I'd really miss the London club scene. But hey! — couldn't I do the job from Head Office in Berkeley Square ?

(d) Okay, okay, I'll take 10 per cent less!

6. Do you think it's possible to be a working woman *and* a mother ?

(a) As long as there are adequate creche facilities, I see no problem.

(b) I 'm sorry, I missed that. Could you come a little closer and repeat the question ?

(c) I have a copy of the Sex Discrimination Act in my briefcase. Would you like to borrow it ?

8. What are your weaknesses ?

(a) I'm too much of a perfectionist. It's terrible, I just can't put something down unless I know it's 110% correct.

(b) (laughing) Can I invoke the right against self-incrimination ?

(c) I'm sadistic, bestial and have necrophiliac tendencies. I've been in therapy for two years now, and it's as bad as ever. Sometimes I think I'm flogging a dead horse.

8. What kind of salary would you be looking for ?

(a) Oh, anything in the £20,000 — £50,000 range.

(b) Salary is a secondary consideration for me. What I'm looking for is challenge and the opportunity to grow as a person.

(c) Whatever you offer, plus 20 per cent.

(d) Twenty grand, eighteen if it's cash in hand, know what I mean ?

9. What would your answer be if I offered you the job right now ?

(a) (Jumps up from chair) Yes! Yes! They said it wasn't possible, but I've proved them wrong! I've done it! (starts blubbering and pumping interviewer's hand).

(b) I don't believe in deciding important issues like this on the spur of the moment. Give me five minutes to think about it.

(c) Fantastic ! Your offer will be worth at least £5000 in my salary bargaining with Price Waterhouse next week.

Interviews are no time to be shy. Employers
appreciate assertiveness in their trainees.

"I WALKED INTO MY INTERVIEW COLD."

An applicant's true confession

"So, Mr Brewster, why do you want to work for us ?"

I eyed the man on the other side of the desk intently. "It takes more than a well-pressed suit and clean fingernails to get a job with us, laddie" was what he really meant. I had interviews lined up with seven other firms that day, and I silently hoped that not all my interrogators would be like Mr Happy sitting before me.

It was then that it dawned on me. I hadn't a clue which firm I was at. Here I was, supposedly keen to spend the rest of my working life with his outfit, and I couldn't even remember its name. I squirmed and turned pale. In all, I had interviews with fifty different firms lined up. Which one was this ?

"Mr Brewster ? I asked you why you want to work for us ?"

I was determined not to lose my composure. If I'd learned any-

thing from listening to Andrew Neil's radio talk-show, it was not to shy away from subjects on which I was completely ignorant.

"For the same reason anyone with my interests would want to work for you, Mr Wills " I grinned. "Because you're one of the real innovators in this industry, that's why !"

He looked puzzled. "An innovator ? To be honest, I've never heard us being called that before."

Not an innovator !? Clearly the company must be in some traditional industry stagnated by complacent attitudes and outmoded working practices. Publishing, maybe.

His eyes narrowed. "Perhaps you'd like to summarise your qualifications for the position ?"

Publishing. It must have been that editorial job with Northern & Shell I had applied for. Appalling pay, but the perks were meant to be unusually good.

"I've always had a respect for your products. In my view they are far more than mere titillation — they serve an important social function which—"

"Titillation ?" he cried. His expression was one of incredulity. Damn. What could it be ? Maybe it was that off-the-wall job with the Nursing Home group I had applied for. It was worth a try.

"You will see on my CV that I spent three months on Operation Raleigh, where I learned how to feed a crew of 26 on a budget of 46p per head per day. I imagine that would prove useful in your business."

"I'm sorry, Mr Brewster, I don't see what you're getting at" he said with disbelief. There was silence. It grew oppressive. I started to laundry-list my abilities:

"My sociology thesis was on the manipulation of consumer behaviour in Western society."

Silence.

Not Sainsbury's then.

"I'm very punctual."

Silence.

Cross out Eurotunnel.

"I'm an optimist."

Silence.

Not that marketing job for Sir Clive Sinclair's solar-powered submarine.

"I don't like coffee."

Nothing.

Not even the Pancreas Foundation.

"I've developed a new computer program that predicts share prices with unprecedented accuracy."

"Is that right ?" he said with the barest hint of interest. "Give me an example of a recent forecast."

"Well, it's been telling me to sell Lonrho short for some time now."

He leaned forward, suddenly intense. "Did you say Lonrho ?"

"Yes. My computer says it's going to hit 28p by the end of the year."

He beamed. "Mr Brewster, you've got the job. " He buzzed his secretary on the internal phone. "Pat, bring me in a copy of the standard House of Fraser employment contract, would you ?"

STRATEGIC WARDROBE MANAGEMENT

THERE IS NO DOUBT AT ALL that clothes are an important factor in business success: there are very few naked people in the upper echelons of corporate life. Just by wearing clothes you score strongly over those who don't.

But it doesn't end there. You may personally feel that the hardy perennials of your wardrobe — the John Collier zipped blouson, the green corduroy maxi-skirt — have a timeless elegance which mere vagaries of fashion cannot eradicate. But you're not the one that needs to be impressed, are you ?

The wise business executive soon realises that the difference between a properly-tailored suit, and one with lapels like a Vulcan bomber, is not just a matter of sartorial taste; it can be the difference between a career in the fast lane and one stuck on the hard-shoulder.

But what exactly should you wear ? For men, all the manuals prescribe a highly conservative and standardised 'uniform', with minor variations for various business sub-cultures. This isn't quite as limiting as it sounds : your suits can run the whole gamut from navy blue to black,with occasional pin-stripes thrown in for added splash. They can be single-breasted, double-breasted, turned-up on the trouser-leg or not turned-up. In fact there are at least 17 different permutations of acceptable styling. In an average office, that means there shouldn't be more than four other people wearing exactly the same suit as you.

Add shirts to the equation, and the variety increases further: they can be white or blue, plain or striped. (If someone in sunglasses tries to sit on you, your stripes are probably a little too wide and bold; if they ask you where your chainsaw is, consider reserving that chequed number you got from Millets for weekend log-splitting.)

Ties should be in understated patterns and preferably in colours that appear in nature. Shoes never anything other than black or dark brown. Studiously avoid anything with built-up heels, buckles or two-tone designs, even if they *are* in Church's sale at the unbelievable knock-down price of £98.00.

Another way to define the right look is by reference to what it is *not*. Take a stroll down the High Street and you will still find lots of fawn suits, short-sleeved pale green shirts with matching ties, light grey shoes with lateral ribbing and 'cushioned' soles. Who buys them is a complete mystery. It should *remain* a mystery as far as you are concerned, and if you find yourself drawn to these items you have a real problem. They are about as acceptable in a professional business environment as a Mohican haircut.

Recent books on business dress have been touting the phrase 'Investment Clothing' : one's wardrobe, so it goes, is nothing more than a portfolio of clothing investments, and decisions about what to wear should be made in the same way you would make decisions about your bonds and equities : some styles are a *buy,* some are a *hold,* and some are a *sell.* You should manage your portfolio to maximise its power value. This might mean, for instance, that it's time to get rid of those shoes which you wore in the snow last year and which now have a salt line stretching round them like a tidal mark. It might mean mothballing your flared suit trousers and patent shoes until the Tom Jones look comes back in again. It might mean expanding your position in button-down Oxford shirts.

The problem with 'dressing for success' is that (a) most people have the basic uniform pretty well figured-out, and (b) there is a limit to how far the formula can be refined. What we mean by this second point is that, just as there is a fashion floor through which you must not fall, so there is a fashion ceiling on which you should avoid bumping your head.

You may simply *love* what Issy Miyake does with soft fabrics. You might think the way Jean-Paul Gaultier cuts jackets is immensely flattering to your bottle-of-claret shoulders. Your Boss blazer might draw looks of admiration and envy down at the Golf Club— but if you turn up at work looking like you've walked off the pages of Esquire, you just won't be taken seriously. Chiselled jaws, sun tans and broad shoulders are very outré in the corporate world — at least, this side of Dallas, they are.

To some extent, discussion of which clothes to wear is otiose. This is because, in recent years, the battle-ground for sartorial dominance has shifted away from clothes, pure and simple, to the more subtle insignias of rank — *power accessories*. Below we list some of the more important ones.

Power Accessory No. 1
The Briefcase

The single most important accessory for any businessman is the leather lunch-box or briefcase. It, more than any other accessory, identifies you as a decision-maker or decision-taker.

To Carry or not to carry

Given how much a good brief-case costs, you might be tempted to do without one until you can cover it in no more than a month's salary. That's fine, but be aware that if you *don't* carry one, people will make one of two assumptions : (a) that you are so low on the corporate ladder that your autonomy is limited to setting the darkness control on the photocopier, or (b) that you are so *high* up the ladder that someone else carries your documents around for you.

Give some thought to which assumption people are likely to make about you. (Clue : don't bank on (a) if you are 22, too skint to have the flapping sole of your shoe glued back on, and in the habit of rolling your own smokes.)

If, despite our advice, you insist on allocating your tight budget to food and shelter before a briefcase, at least carry a folded copy of the Financial Times to and from work to signal your daily communion with Mammon.

Style

The briefcase is one of the few business accessories for which bigger is not necessarily better. Only the business underclass carry accordion-style cases large enough to take a full set of The Encyclopaedia Britannica.* Upper-level decision-makers deal only in one-page memos.

Choosing just the right case requires great care. We suggest something made of genuine belting leather,

*Note their popularity with lawyers

simple in design, of rigid frame construction, and in dark brown. Put your initials on it if you like, but have them burned on, not tooled in gold, and make sure the letters do not exceed 3/8 inch high.

Power Acessory No. 2
The Portable Computer

Given that many of today's top businessmen were schooled in a period when complex calculations were carried out with the help of Napier's Logarithms, and when the only people who went *near* a typewriter keyboard were those funny chaps who wore lipstick and danced backwards, the inroads which personal computers have made into executive life have been very rapid indeed.

British executives took to desktops faster than almost any other European country, and, as for their refined cousins — the portables — there are currently over 130 models on the market.

When the first portables came out, it was something of a labour of love to own one: they were big, heavy and about as much fun to lug around as one of those six-foot diameter oak collars that prisoners in the Middle Ages had to wear. Technical advancements have made those early models virtually valueless. The lat-

est machines weigh in at a bantam 6lb, run for up to ten hours between battery recharges, and have enough memory to swallow a good chunk of the British Library. They also run on simpler and better software : programs that required you to type <Doc>50/@/Acc. to access a file have been replaced by user-friendly windows that even complete techno-peasants can understand.

What this has meant is that the portable computer has become a genuinely useful business tool. Whether you want to calculate the imputed cost of capital on a multi-million pound sale-and-leaseback deal, or fit in a quick round on St. Andrews Old Course between meetings, you can do it with the help of a 486 Intel chip.

Hand in hand with technical advances have come brand distinctions. If you're about to buy a portable, don't assume that like-for-like brands all have the same clout and that people won't sneer at you if you have the wrong one. They don't and they will.

Size

The first point to take on board is that it's not what you do with it that's important. Size is what matters. Basically, the lighter and more compact your unit, the better. Anything made before 1990 is likely to have the dimensions and weight of an old portable typewriter and be called a 'laptop' — a strange nomenclature given the dangers of having one on your lap without wearing knee-strengtheners and an earthed cricket box.

Later evolutions of the product are known as 'Notebooks' and do indeed live up to their name, being little bigger than a pad of A4 paper. In the macho world of portable computers, these beasts are the ones to have. If you do have one, never ever refer to it as a laptop. That would be no less immodest than describing your Ferrari as a hatchback. It's a notebook, and make people aware of that fact.

Speed

If you plan to crunch net present values to the tune of seven figures on your portable PC, and don't want to trip over your beard waiting for the result, make sure you get one with the right chip. Chips are what determine the computer's speed, and the dominant chip manufacturer is Intel.

Early PCs used the Intel 286. Compared to later chips, this is an evolutionary throwback —interesting as a museum piece, but of no modern-day relevance. If anyone tries to sell you a machine which uses one, or a colleague boasts about his 286-processor portable, feel free to treat them to a generous portion of humble pie.

A few years after the 286 came the 386 — considerably faster and, until last year, the one to be seen with. Not any more : now you don't want to be seen with anything but a 486. In fact, by the time you read this, you should already be talking about replacing it with Intel's new generation of chip — the *Pentium*. Okay, so they haven't developed it yet, but don't let that worry you.

Memory

The third great indicium of your computer's — and by implication your own — power is its memory. It is like someone asking whether your Sierra is a run-of-the-mill LX or a souped-up Cozzie, or how many bedrooms your house has got.

The joy is that you don't need to understand how memory works to be able to hold forth on the subject, and no-one can tell if you're telling the truth anyway because the guts of the machine are on the inside.

Memory is all about acronyms, of which the following are the most important : *RAM, ROM, SIMMS, BIT & K*. Don't worry about what they stand for. People who know their *ROMS* from their *RAMS* (like you) never use their full names. All you have to remember is that your machine has a *ROM* of at least 4 and a

RAM of at least 40. Anything less is Mickey-Mouse stuff. Go as high as 16 and 200 respectively if you really want to impress your audience, but be prepared for awkward questions along the lines of "Wow, I didn't know you could get more than 5 SIMMS into an Amstrad PC9256. How did you do it ?"

If you ever find your bluff being called in this way, try to stifle or deflect the line of questioning : "Oh, I could bang on for hours about memory, but you don't want to hear that. How is Jane by the way ?" Alternatively switch into anecdotal mode : "You know, back in the 60's they had computers the size of a room which could only store a single sentence; now a fingernail-sized chip can store the Oxford Dictionary. Incredible, isn't it ?" Delivered with a judicious hint of first-hand knowledge, this sort of off-the-cuff remark can be just as impressive as any amount of techno-babble.

So . . . Size, Speed and Memory, the three key words in PC one-upmanship. If someone starts a conversation on computers, your aim should be to get in and out with a lightning strike that leaves your audience in thrall to your expertise without daring to ask more. If the conversation goes on for more than three sentences, you'll be out of your depth in no time. Stick to generalisations, casual remarks,

hints, and conversation stoppers and you'll be safe enough.

Power Accessory No. 3
The Pocket Diary

Over the last five years there has been such a lot of publicity for *electronic* diaries like the Psion Organiser and the Sharp pocket computer, you could almost forget that, for the common herd, it is the ordinary bound diary that acts as the appointments clearing house.

As the lowest common denominator of corporate giftware, the desk diary lacks the necessary exclusivity for real image-leverage — unless, that is, yours is a personal present from the Sultan of Brunei, hand-stitched in Connolly hide and tooled in gold-leaf. A run-of-the-mill page-a-day job with your accountant's name stuck on the cover isn't going to bowl anyone over and is best left where its name implies it should be : propping up a short leg.

In fact, it is arguable that the diary has no place at all in the power accessory portfolio. After all, a sought-after, time-pressured, decision-maker never *sees* his diary, far less makes an entry in it. "Have a word with my secretary Frances. She'll tell you if I'm free" has to be the the all-time executive power-play, particularly if the appointment in question is no more than six hours away.

There are still occasions, however, when conspicuous consultation of a pocket diary can boost your credibility rating. Imagine that you're dining with an influential business acquaintance and, in the course of the conversation, you want to make a brief note of some tip he's given you — his mother's recipe for Hollandaise Sauce, perhaps, or the number of someone in the Met who can have your accumulated £1,150 of parking tickets wiped clean.

Whipping out a vinyl 99p notebook with shreds of paper hanging off its spiral just won't do, any more than you would sign a prestigious business agreement with a one-inch pencil pulled from behind your ear. Certain observable standards are called for. That's where your pocket diary comes into play. Not one with separate sections for "Blondes", "Brunettes" and "Redheads", nor one with coloured dividers labelled "Things to do" and "Personal Finances". (The very idea that finances of your complexity could be encapsulated in anything less than four looseleaf binders should be abhorrent to you.) No, what you want is something dark, slim and elegant from Smythsons in Bond Street. They're expensive for what they are, but it's worth paying the extra.

There are two other reasons why you should carry a diary. You never know when you'll want to get out of an undesired invitation, and producing a well-filled diary lends credibility to your weasly excuses, as in "I hate to postpone again John, but look — I'm booked solid until a year from September."

Finally, a diary is probably the only way to work out at the end of the year what the hell you'be been doing for the previous twelve months.

Power Accessory No. 4
The Pale Complexion

Although there are undeniable social advantages in having a healthy tan, success in a business environment mandates an entirely different set of priorities: to look anything but sallow and baggy-eyed, especially during your first few years in the field, is to invite suspicion that you just haven't got enough work to keep you busy at the weekend. That can be fatal to a career, and you should always groom yourself to look hard-driven (without looking totally knackered). Your aim is to cultivate the reputation of a workhorse (let your colleagues think that you wouldn't *ever* go to bed but for social reasons) and to be known as the 'can-do' guy — the person to be relied upon when the going gets tough.

In this quest, as in many others, appearance is more important than reality. If you've ever seen a junior doctor who's just come off Casualty after an unbroken 36-hour shift, you'll have some idea of the benchmark.

Bear in mind that if you are ever press-ganged into working an all-nighter, you have a fantastic opportunity to tweak your image up a notch or two. Work your shift with ease and nonchalance, and news of your stamina will soon spread, while the half-inch stubble on your chin next morning will provide impressive visual evidence of your heroic capacity for toil (particularly on women).

The perils of a tan in this context are obvious. Or to be more accurate, the perils of an **all-year-round** tan are obvious. Everybody takes a holiday once in a while and it's only to be expected that you should come back looking a little bit healthier than when you left. What is not acceptable is topping up that tan artificially so that you look like an Aztec sun god in mid-November. Apart from anything else, it is a painfully transparent artifice when you left the office only the previous evening with standard English alabaster.

If you *insist* on using a sunlamp, at least take the following precautions :

(a) Only brown yourself at weekends. That way, if the office wiseguy remarks on the sudden appearance of a tan, you can at least fabricate some story about having acquired it over a bracing 36 holes at Sandwich.

(2) During the Winter, wear ski goggles while lying under the lamp. The white area around your eyes will help corroborate your story about having spent the weekend shcussing through nine inches of fresh powder in Val D'Isere on your Fat Boys.

(3) It is a proven fact that excessive use of your sunlamp beyond maximum suggested exposure times can lead to premature executive burn-out.

Power Accessory No. 5
The Business Card

The business card is a concise statement of your corporate identity. listing your name, firm, business address, title and telephone number. The style of your card will depend considerably on the business you are in, but whatever business that is, there are a few groundrules to observe :

1. Avoid pretentious job titles such as "Lord of the Realm, De-

fender of the Faith, Keeper of the Truth" or "Director of Corporate Planning".

2. Exercise modesty in choosing the printed size of your name.

3. Raised print radiates more power than flat print. Flat print radiates more power than photocopied print.

4. Stick with heavy 100 per cent rag white or ecru stock, and standard ink colours.

5. Steer clear of trite business slogans like "Everyone likes to feel kneaded" if you run a bakery, or "Our Business is always Picking up" if you're in refuse collection.

6. Don't put your home phone number on the card if you value your marriage.

The discrimination which you show in distributing your cards is also important, the general rule being that the more generous you are, the less they will be valued. Many young executives are so proud of their first card that they dispense them the same way new fathers dispense cigars, spitting them out with the speed and dexterity of a top Vegas croupier. This is bad form. Wait until the conclusion of a business discussion to exchange cards. You can then add a personalised touch before handing yours over — by, for instance, scribbling down your pri-

vate number at the office, or the number of your Swiss bank account.

Power Accessory No. 6
The Executive Pen

Because the pen is mightier than the sword, it is worth choosing your weapon with some care. Nothing will stain your cultivated image of business polish more quickly than signing a billion-pound debt deal with a masticated Pentel.

The sensible course is to raid the company stationery cupboard for biros and fibre tips to use in your ordinary work, but keep something glitzy for those occasions when what is required is more than just a device for transferring ink to the page. Unfortunately, many otherwise decent brands have lost their exclusivity and become commodities of the corporate gift market, which means that if you really want to impress, you have to flee upmarket to the ultimate in ostentatious vulgarity : Mont Blanc or Waterman.

Note that it is *impossible* to impress with a ball point pen however prestigious its badging. In senior management circles fountain pens are de rigueur. This will come as unwelcome news to those who last used an ink pen at school — and then with all the dexterity of a shipyard riveter on The Generation Game required to ice a wedding cake. Nevertheless, make an effort — and stock up on blotch.

The colour of ink you put in your pen is also significant. Avoid offbeat or bohemian colours like red, green, or (worst of all) brown. High-fliers use dark blue and black only.

Keep your pen in your briefcase or the inside pocket of your jacket. Never clip it in the breast pocket of your jacket — a style popular with TV repairmen and mining engineers, but not at board level. Don't abuse your pen by chewing it or by playing the drum solo from *'Stairway to Heaven'* during meetings. If you have to cover up your nerves, tap it lightly on your lips while looking thoughtful. It will make others think you are generating very deep corporate strategy.

Power Accessory No. 7
The Signature

The two most important words you will ever write as a business executive — and eventually the *only* two words you will ever physically write yourself as a senior executive — are your first and second names. Your signature is your personal logo, and you need to give as much thought to its initial deisgn and on-going modification as the designers at Slough do to the Mars Bar wrapper.

A properly thought-out signature will express your drive and energy, certainly — but it should also show sensitivity to your position in the corporate hierarchy. This means it should evolve as you get promoted in your firm. A completely illegible signature would be pretentious for a junior marketing trainee, whereas an artlessly legible one would be immature for someone on the Board.

On the opposite page we show how the signature of one executive — Alfred Stern — evolved as he advanced up the corporate ladder.

Power Accesory No. 8
The Credit Card

In the late 1980's the exclusive image of credit cards evaporated, as banks and high street chains junk-sold their cards through every mailing database except the old boys list of the Scrubs. The predictable result, given that the only plastic most of the punters had ever handled before was a Top Rank Bingo Card, was to stimulate a spiralling and uncontrollable credit boom. This involved card-holders raiding Dixons

EVOLUTION OF AN
EXECUTIVE SIGNATURE

Year		*Career Position*
1946		Hired as warehouse assistant aged 16. Not allowed to sign anything except Goods In slips. Swirly underlining draws rude remarks from lorry drivers.
1950		Promoted to salesman. Adds last name to make contracts legal, and new nickname to make customers think of him as their friend.
1955		Promoted to area sales manager. Switches to full first name to add dignity. Signature still somewhat legible, but shows more maturity and determination. Clearly a man to watch.
1963		Sent to sort out sales of North American subsidiary. Use of middle name reflects desire to blend in with American business culture, and secret ambition to become Managing Director.
1970		Promoted to Sales Director of Group. Uses initials to save precious time; legibility decreases correspondingly.
1984		Managing Director. Signing 30 documents a day. Initials only. Growth in size of signature directly proportional to growth in ego.
1993		Chairman of the Board. Returns to full signature as pressure eases. Scrawl now completely illegible. Often confused with his electro-cardiogram

for a tower stereo system, when they couldn't have plonked down **cash** for the plug to go on the end of it.

The card companies are a little bit more fussy nowadays about who touts their plastic, but only a little bit. Anyone can build up some kind of credit-card collection, just by launching an application blitz on the High Street chains. Admittedly, a Woolies card won't buy you the finer things in life, but it *will* (along with a few months of solid work experience and a positive bank balance) allow you to leverage up to the next tier of plastic : Visa, Access or even to American Express .

This is bad news for the ambitious high-flier seeking to distance himself or herself from the *hoi poloi*. If everyone can get a green Amex, what do the elites use ? Well, there are two things you can do :

(i) upgrade to something hardly anyone else has got : either one of the prestigious cards where everyone *knows* you need an enormous income to qualify — Amex *Gold* , for instance — or get yourself a card from some obscure provincial Swiss bank, where people will assume that only you and Mark Rich could

satisfy the eligibility requirement.

(ii) snip up all your cards and carry cash. In the right quantities, this can be no less impressive than even the biggest-hitting credit card. e.g. when you pay for that seven bedroom Georgian house by snapping open the combination locks on your briefcase and laying out bundles of fifties in neat rows.

Cash, you see, still means something, whereas credit doesn't. No-one knows this better than your bank manager, and if you ever feel the aberrant urge to take him to lunch, make sure you pay by peeling off a couple of twenties from an elasticated roll in your back pocket. This will reassure him that you are, like him, a cash-flow person. Emphasise the point, if you like, by fanning the remaining notes to your ear, and murmuring to yourself "£475 to the end of the month. Still ahead of budget." He will appreciate the touch.

Of course, paying for lunch under any circumstances is an unpleasant affair. For those unfamiliar with the etiquette of credit cards — when to hold 'em, when to fold 'em — refer to the following guide :

CREDIT CARD ETIQUETTE

1. If you *must* use entry-level cards like the basic Access or Visa at a restaurant, don't let your business colleagues find out. Quietly extract your card from your wallet while pretending to check the bill. Then you can hand bill and card to the waiter together without betraying your embarrassingly weak hand. Conversely, if you have a real power card like an Amex Gold or something from Coutts Brothers, play it face-up with polished insouciance.

2. Beware of friends who offer to pay the whole bill on their credit cards while asking you to reimburse them for your share in cash. Their motives may be less than magnanimous. Even with interest rates as low as they now are, the free use of your money, plus the ability to sit on the bill for 30 days until the statement comes in, will yield an annualised return of over 11 per cent *after tax*. This gambit is currently the rage among City fund managers, most of whom can't manage *pre-tax* yields of more than 5 per cent from conventional investments like equities or bonds.

3. If you are caught short at a business meeting without a prestige card, *never* admit it. Reach *slowly* for your wallet, allowing your companions to get their cards out first. Alternatively, pre-empt the competition with a declaration like "I don't believe in plastic money. The consumer credit explosion of the 80's has a lot to answer for." It's sanctimonious, but better than being humiliated.

4. The best investment of all is to pay cash and to demand a 3 or 4 per cent discount from the restaurant. Remember, businesses have to pay credit card companies a tariff of between 4 and 7 per cent off the top of all bills. They should be prepared to cut you in on the extra profits they earn by accepting cash. If they object, remind them that sterling notes are still legal tender backed by the full faith and credit of the Bank of England, and accepted in over fifty million retail outlets throughout the world.

5. Be careful not to overextend yourself : a newspaper recently carried the story of a young man who diligently and legally collected over 1,500 credit cards, carrying a combined credit line in excess of £1 million. His annual salary was £14,000. Imagine how well you could do.

TRICKS OF
THE TRADE

OFFICE POLITICS
and ETIQUETTE

IN THE REAL WORLD, THE ONLY thing that counts is performance — *recent* performance. Anything that happened before the close of the last quarter is ancient history, But while cutting costs, increasing market share, reducing employee turnover, and being top goal-scorer in the office hockey team will all count in your favour, they are not enough. This is because when a company evaluates executive performance, *perception* is often more important than *reality*. You might be slogging your guts out and doing a first-class job, but if someone else is taking all the credit, you'll never rise above second-rate jobs like vice-president.

On the following pages are some hints about how to project the right image. We start with the most common (and if you've got any sense the most intimate) form of physical contact you will experience with working colleagues : the handshake.

Lesson One :
Moving and Shaking

First impressions *are* important. The handshake is your first line of offence when meeting colleagues and clients. There are many kinds of handshakes used in business, and it is important to master as many of them as possible. Consult the following guide to expand your current repertoire, and improve your ability to "read" the handshakes you receive.

1. The Straight Shake

With the Straight Shake, hands meet fully extended, lock, and clasp with moderate pressure for no more than three seconds.

This is the classic shake, what you might call the international standard for businessmen everywhere.

"You may well be the top fee-earner in the firm, Dodds, but don't blow your trumpet too loud, there's a good chap."

2. The Twofer Shake

This hearty shake was originally exclusive to politicians out on the hustings, but has regrettably started to make an appearance in business circles.

It starts off like a Straight Shake but is reinforced with a blind-side attack by the left hand. As a recipient, you will find your hand suddenly gripped on both sides by the greeter, effectively depriving you of all further control.

The Twofer is much favoured at business conventions, where executives indulge in a charade of exaggerated camaraderie with anyone who looks even vaguely capable of putting some business their way.

3. The Shakedown

The Shakedown is used instinctively by young public school stockbrokers who have been brought up to believe that a limp handshake is a certain sign of moral weakness and sexual deviancy. They would rather *die* than deliver one, and, to make sure there is no mistake, they turn every introduction into the most excrutiating form of hand-to-hand combat. For the recipient, it is like being given a tourniquet.

In technique the Shakedown is similar to the Straight Shake except for the intensity of application and the more extended duration. To perform it, first work out with a wrist-exerciser for several months. When you're strong enough to squeeze droplets of oil from a handful of walnuts, you're ready. Give your opponent a solid six-count before delivering the release.

4. The Golden Handshake

This shake is particularly effective in dealings with African trade ministries or Lambeth council

5. The Masonic Shake

No-one quite knows what this shake involves except that, if used in the right circles, it can smooth the path to that lucrative contract/job/bonus. Reputedly, some form of digit play and a hoisted trouser leg is involved, but if you are thinking of giving it a try, do be selective about the when and the where. Tickling your interviewer's palm with your forefinger may raise an entirely different set of issues to those you have in mind.

Other Options

Those who find the handshake needlessly formal occasionally opt for an embrace, a kiss on both cheeks, or a pat on the back. The embrace or kiss should be used sparingly, but it is safe in France and other developing nations.

Women executives are constantly confronted with male counterparts who are unsure whether to kiss, shake, or use some other form of greeting. If you do not want to be kissed, extend your hand when your opponent is still at least five feet away and offer him the Straight Shake. If he ignores your signals and tries to kiss you anyway, stop him cold with a bone-crushing Shakedown.

Each of these variant techniques has its place in the business world. If you find yourself in unfamiliar surroundings or are in any doubt whatsoever, choose the low-risk strategy and deliver the Straight Shake.

Lesson Two : How to Make the Right Small Talk

Small talk is a big factor in business success: it's bad form to be caught with nothing to say, and people expect something a little more sophisticated than discussion of whether Bunny is going to be written out of *Eldorado*.

That said, the first rule of business conversation is: **don't sound too intellectual**. Not many business leaders have picked up prizes in Stockholm, and if you come on strong with monologues on Hegelian metaphysics or next year's Booker candidates, you'll only raise eyebrows. No-one is saying that you can't be interested in such things in the privacy of your own home. Just don't bring them to the office. Sounding *au courant* with intellectual or artistic matters in a business context is about as acceptable as openly talking about making a fortune out of text books if you're a University professsor.

If you can't talk about your real interests, what can you talk about ?

Confine yourself to discussion of the weather, last weekend, this weekend, parking tickets, the spouse and children, wine, holidays, mortgages, and good films you've seen lately (if you can think of any). Articles in *Marketing Week, Business Age* or the *FT* are always good bets. Avoid mentioning subjects like your ex-spouse, your 9 year-old son's joyriding problem ("They do say he's good . . . "), the fact that you *still* haven't paid your poll tax and what a laugh that is, the continuing depression affecting your industry, your salary, and the meaning of corporate life.

Acceptable Business Books
(i) Anything with the word 'Strategy' or 'Quality' in the title;

(ii) *Accounting for Growth* by Terry Smith (unless your company features in it)

(iii) *The Zulu Principle* by Jim Slater.

Unnacceptable Business Books
(i) Anything that might lead your superiors to believe that your business skills weren't acquired naturally eg. *'How to Develop Charisma and Personal Magnetism'*

(ii) Anything that might lead your superiors to believe that your luxury lifestyle wasn't acquired legally: *How to Lead a Better Life by Stealing Office Supplies* by Dogbert;

(iii) This book.

Acceptable Non-Business magazines to be seen reading : *The Spectator, Private Eye, Vogue* (Italian edition), *The Sporting Life, Yachting World, The Modern Review, The Oldie, The Haiku Quarterly* (or something else equally obscure).

Unnacceptable Non-Business Magazines to be seen Reading : , , *Hello, For Women, Bunty, Practical Parenting, The Big Issue, Caravan World, Kerrang!*

Lesson Three
Cheap Talk

Now that you know *what* to talk about, you need to focus on the medium through which most of your business conversations will take place. Bell's invention puts every executive within a finger's reach of every other executive — a true boon if you are trying to sell advertising space in the 'Opportunity Bulgaria!' directory, a true bane if you are the unhappy recipient of such calls.

Executive telephony is the body of elaborate strategies which business executives use to screen unwanted calls, and the equally re-

sourceful counter-strategies which theu use to penetrate an opponent's expert screening. On the following pages is a brief summary of the main techniques involved

---

Defensive Strategies

1. Your secretary is instructed to obtain the name and company of the caller, and the purpose of the call.

2. She puts the caller on hold, and relays the information to you. You decide whether to take the call, or have it "terminated with extreme prejudice".

3. If the call is from an irate creditor, a pensions salesman, or your mother-in-law, tell your secretary to reply with one of the following defensive misrepresentations :

(a) "Ms Stevens is in a meeting."

(b) "Ms Stevens is on another call, and I have two more waiting. Would you like to hold ?"

(c) "Ms Stevens has left for the day."

(d) "Ms Stevens no longer works here."

(e) "I'm sorry, Ms Stevens died last week after a long bout of jet lag."

If you want to maintain some sort of future relationship with the caller, return the call at around 1:15 when there's a good chance he or she will be out at lunch. Leave a message that you returned the call, and instruct your secretary to use a different defensive strategy when the caller calls again after lunch.

Offensive Strategies

Not so long ago, telemarketing companies required only one quality of their employees : a nice middle-class accent. Even if you were so thick that all you needed to survive was medium light and watering twice a week, you could get a job. The right voice would get you past the secretary and give you a shot at the boss.

Today's secretaries are more savvy and less impressionable. Defensive barriers have become more difficult to breach and the offensive strategies required to penetrate them correspondingly more extreme. Nevertheless, with the right tactics and a little luck, it *is* still possible to pitch the Chairman of ICI on the company toilet paper account, completely cold. Consider the following two dialogues involving you and Sir Denys Henderson's secretary.

A. The Pussyfoot Approach

The phone is answered on the third ring . . . .

CM : "Catherine Myers speaking. Can I help you ?"

You : "Good morning, I wonder if I could speak with Sir Denys Henderson ?"

CM : "May I ask who is speaking ?"

You : "Yes. My name is Ian Williams, and I'm calling from the London Toilet Tissue Comapny"

CM (*Challenging*) : "Does Sir Denys know you Mr Williams ?"

You : "Er . . .well no, but—"

CM : "May I ask the purpose of your call ?"

You : "Well, I was hoping that he could spare me a few minutes regarding your company's office sanitation acc–"

CM "I'm sorry Mr Williams, Sir Denys is on another call. Can I suggest you call Group Logistics on 081 493 5684. Goodbye."

B. The Rottweiler Approach

The phone is answered on the third ring . . . .

CM : "Catherine Myers speaking. Can I help you ?"

You : "Denys Henderson please."

CM : "May I ask who's speaking ?"

You (abruptly) "Ian Williams."
CM : "Does Sir Denys know you Mr Williams ?"

"I'm sorry — he's tied up with some gentlemen from Cork Gully."

Ignore the question. Allow a pause for a few seconds, then start barking "Denys ? Denys ? Are you there ?"

CM (a little intimidated) : "May I ask the purpose of your call, Sir ?"

You (impatiently) "It's an urgent matter to do with your company's waste management programme."

This should be enough to browbeat even the most hardened of PAs into submission. If, however, you feel even greater force is required to penetrate the perimeter fence, work in some heavy sarcasm :

CM : "May I ask the purpose of your call, Sir ?"

YOU : "Oh, for God's sake, I want to sell him some bog rolls, what do you think ! Just put me through !"

It's ballistic, but it does the trick. In exceptional circumstances, you may have to exercise drastic economy with the truth using one of the following ploys :

You : (in an obscure middle-European accent) : "Atlantis Clinic. Eet's a private matter." (Cheap and underhand, but effective.)

or, *in extremis*

"This is his stockbroker. I've got some bad news, and it is imperative that I speak to him before the market closes."

Ending a Call

You don't have to be a guru of time management to know that rambling phone calls are public enemy number one when it comes to whitecollar producvtivity.

Just because the person on the other end of the line has nothing better to do with his time than rant on about Network South East doesn't mean you have to stay on the line.

If you find yourself on the receiving end of an unsolicited monologue, you should first try to terminate it by subtle and graceful means. This isn't always possible. You mya have to use one of the five other ways to get yourself off the hook, listed here in decreasing order of politeness.

1. "Bill, I'd love to talk more about this, but I know you're a busy man so I'll let you go."

2. "Bill, that's my other line. I'd better go. I'll give you a call next week."

3. (Accompanied by groans of pain) "Damn ! My ulcers are playing up again. Sorry Bill, I've got to dash out for some Tagamet."

4. "Listen, I'm getting a bleeper saying there are people holding on the line — let me put you on low-priority hold."

5. Hang up in mid-sentence. When the caller calls you back, tell your secretary to blame a technical fault and say you had to dash out for a meeting.

Lesson Four :
Drink for Success

Though an occasional executive is heard to express regret at becoming a cog in a corporate machine, most find solace in the fact that Great Britain Ltd is at least a well-oiled machine. Alcohol is a *sine qua non* of business life, with most deals being discussed over a beer and closed over a glass of champagne. In business or out, it helps to have a drink before getting into bed with a total stranger. That said, you should be aware of the strict conventions regarding business drinking :

Rules of Successful Business Drinking

1. Remember that as a business executive you are a *decision-maker*. Abdicating responsibility by ordering the house brand of whisky suggests that you are completely undiscriminating, and is tantamount to admitting you wear Fruit of the Loom underwear. Better to affect a degree of savoir faire by ordering a Glenlivet on the rocks — especially when the bill comes and your drinking partner sees that it cost you £6 a shot.

2. Avoid boozing before breakfast, except at conventions.

3. Men should avoid ordering any of the following in the early running: Zombie, Harvey Wallbanger, Purple Jesus.

4. Women should avoid ordering any of the following during the late running: Double Martini, Samoan War God, Sloe Comfortable Screw Up Against The Wall.

5. It is okay to show some prejudice against watery foreign lagers and to extol the virtues of good English bitter, but exercise some tact and restraint: if you're pitching for the £500,000 advertising account of the Canadian Tourist Board you won't help your cause by recounting your Moosehead lager joke: Q: "How do you know if a man likes Moosehead ?" A: "He's got antler marks on his stomach."

6. It is quite acceptable to show a healthy disdain for French wines, especially when in the company of a French client. e.g. "What I always wonder about Piat D'Or is how they get the cat to squat over the bottle." If you say it fast enough he won't understand, but your colleagues will, and they'll love you for it.

7. Trying to match the office dipso round-for-round will do wonders for your reputation in the Post Room. If you want to be in on their lunchtime drinking sesh, that is your prerogative, but don't expect an invitation to the Director's dining room once the word gets round.

8. In negotiations, always drink less than your opposite number, especially when it looks like turning into a marathon afternoon. If you're sensible, you'll be the first to switch to mineral water or Campari.

9. Total abstinence is regarded as suspicious in the business world. If your idea of a good drink is a pot of lime blossom tea, think twice about ordering it when everyone else is hell bent on oblivion. Order something with oomph — like a triple Jack Daniels on the rocks — but nurse it slowly with plenty of ice.

LUNCHTIME RECREATION
How to Consume Alcohol without Paying for Same

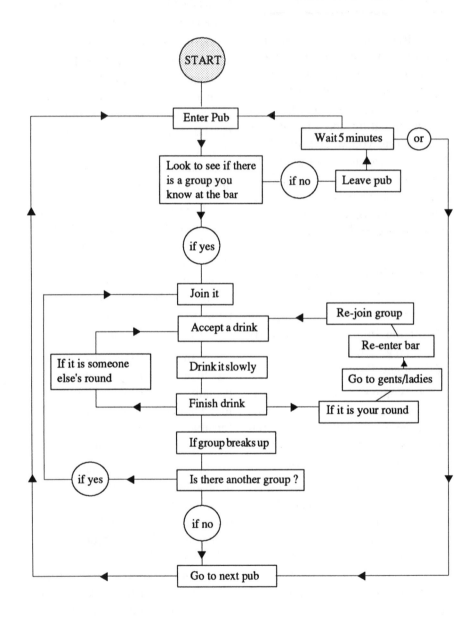

Lesson Five :
Business Air Travel

It may sound glamorous to travel to Paris one week, Amsterdam the next and Chicago the next, but for most business people the attraction of business travel quickly wears off. After two or three flights in a single month you will reach a plateau of boredom, every departure lounge will start to look pretty much like every other departure lounge, and every stewardess pretty much like the back end of the plane.

There are, however, ways to make the travelling treadmill more tolerable :

The Do's and Don'ts of
Business Air Travel

1. **Do** fly First or at least Club class — if you're on an expense account. You'll have more leg room, you'll get somewhat edible food, and you'll be first off the plane. More importantly, you'll meet other movers and shakers of the business world.

2. **Do not** check any baggage into the cargo hold. Ever. It could get lost or stolen. Worst of all, it could cause you to miss a connecting flight. Any business traveller worth his salt can live for two or three weeks out of a single piece of hand baggage. Why do you think business travellers play tennis on their foreign trips .... and leave their golf clubs at home ?

3. **Do** work on the plane instead of drinking vats of booze and wasting time on vacuous in-flight magazines. This is especially true if your fees are hourly-rated, or if the person sitting next to you looks like he is going to show you pictures of his granchildren.

4. **Do not** work openly on confidential company documents, unless you have previously ascertained that the person sitting next to you is blind, a rock-musician on mood-ameliorating drugs, or the unfortunate possessor of a forty-seventh chromosone.

5. **Do** stump up the £100 a year which it costs to join an airline club. Most people still aren't aware of the fact that all big airports have somewhere far more comfortable to park yourself while waiting for a flight than those agonising plastic airport chairs. If you've ever wondered what hidden chamber all those first-class passengers emerge from one minute before take-off, now you know.

6. **Do not** change your watch to local time when crossing time zones, unless you intend to stay for more

*"Geoffrey, do you think the client is
making some kind of point flying Economy?"*

than two days; you'll only get jet lag. Instead, try to eat meals and go to bed in accordance with GMT.

7. **Do** buy airline insurance if you're scared of flying. It may be the worst insurance deal going, but just thinking about that tax-free £250,000 will soothe your nerves when the aeroplane hits a sharp downdraft. Besides, when the insurance company pay-out drops through your post box five weeks later, your spouse will know that you *really* cared.

8. **Do not** waste time at the beginning of the flight watching the flight attendants doing their safety spiel. You'll always have twenty seconds or so to put your Evelyn Wood training to work speed-reading the idiot card while the pilot tries to fly the plane on its one remaining engine. If he fails, and the plane nosedives into the Alps, you're a cooked goose anyway.

9. **Do** ask for a second dinner on a partially empty flight. They won't always oblige, but once in a while you'll get lucky and actually end up with a square meal.

10. **Do not** try to pick up the flight attendants. It may have been years since someone last smiled at you, expressed an interest in your welfare, and tucked you up for the night, but in the case of stewards and stewardesses their concern is purely professional. Every now and then you hear stories . . . but unless you are prepared to face the risk of a very public rejection, we would advise against pitching for membership of the 'Mile-High Club'.

Lesson Six :
How to Survive Muzak

As if we don't get enough piped music in supermarkets, hotel foyers and Indian restaurants, some businesses have started introducing it to the office environment. Lifts, lavatories, and reception areas are the most common areas, but even if *your* business has remained music-free, you can't always avoid the problem : you ring up a friend in a less enlightened office, are put on hold, and immediately subjected to an excrutiating three minutes of Bach's Brandenburg Concerto (Fisher Price variation).

As innocuous as it sounds, Muzak is an insidious agent of subliminal mood control. Businesses use it on the premise that efficiency is enhanced if workers are stimulated by emotional climaxes followed by productive plateaus. On Monday mornings, for example, the first segment will start off with an inspirational piece like the theme from 'Dambusters' or something with a back beat like 'Satisfaction'. This is followed by something to get the office really humming, like 'Raindrops Keep Falling'.

Thankfully, Muzak is generally only found where the challenge of the work is below 11-plus level. As a high-flier, you should not encounter it too often. If the top executives in your company have it piped into *their own* offices, it's time to cash in your share options and hand in your notice. If it is introduced into *your* office, there are four ways to cope :

(a) earplugs
(b) a white noise generator
(c) your own Walkman
(d) playing 'Name that Tune'

'Name that Tune' is suitable for all ages, since the anonymous horns and strings are so hungry for new material, they will homogenise beyond recognition anything from 'Two Little Boys' to a Vanilla Ice rap.

Lesson Seven : Information Technology

The greatest minds in business today are the IBM 3081, the Amdahl 470/V6, the Cray 3, and the Iliac IV. The specifications of these monster computers are staggering :

Speed : billions of calculations per second.
Memory : bigger than Magnus Magnusson
Input/Output : over fifty pages of printout per second
Power Consumption : 1 million watts and upwards
In Use : 23.73 hours per day
Logic : binary

Your office probably won't have one of these nimble leviathans. Instead you'll have a string of networked PCs, smaller but still incredibly powerful, and probably sitting right in front of you on your desk.

Your PC should be more than just a parapet to duck behind when the Boss is prowling around on Friday afternoons looking for bodies to work the weekend. Amazing as it seems, it is there to make your job easier. That's why firms invest millions every year upgrading their hardware. Whether it actually does will depend, to a large extent, on how the I.T. specialist has set up the system : what programs it is running, how your department is linked to other departments, who is allowed access to what information, and so on.

I.T specialists who know what they are doing are, however, comparatively rare. The one helping you out is likely to have the following specifications :

Speed: minimal.
Memory: about 10% of what he needs to do his job.
Input/Output: About 70 spoken words per minute, 5% of which may be relevant.
Power Consumption: 3000 calories per day
In Use: whenever your system crashes.
Logic: random

GRANDON'S LAWS OF INFORMATION TECHNOLOGY

1. If one piece of valuable information is sought from a computer, it will be buried in a 200-page printout.

2. Errors will be discovered in the accounting file only after the backup disc has been erased.

3. When a program prints detailed information, only the summary will be looked at.

4. When a program prints only a summary, detailed information will be sought.

5. Computer bugs are always discovered by the Managing Director.

6. Computer security presents an impenetrable obstacle only to those who are supposed to use the system.

7. Just when you have started to work out how a program works, the I.T. department will insist on upgrading or, worse still, changing to a different one.

8. The one day per month when the computer system crashes will be the one day you really need it.

9. Keying-in errors are never detected until after the cheque has been posted.

10. Grandon's Inequality : the number of I.T. experts + the number of data-processing clerks + the number of maintenance personnel is always greater than the number of people the computer was brought in to replace.

Lesson Eight : Social Events

1. The Christmas Party

For the young executive interested in attaining high-flier status, the annual Christmas bash presents many risks and many opportunities. If you know you have a reputation for being anti-social and boring, it is the one chance in the year to show what a funster you can be, by mingling casually with the support staff and laughing at their jokes. It is also a chance for your spouse to meet your boss's spouse, a chance to forge alliances with colleagues from other departments, and a chance to put on a skit ridiculing your office enemies with impunity.

Warning: Showing your human side is one thing; letting it all hang out is quite another. In many ways, the Christmas party is like a game of musical chairs in which one (or usually two) employees get caught out when the music stops, and become the subject of hilarious stories for the rest of their working lives. Be on your guard : this is not the time to come out of the closet, break your personal best in Moscow Mules, or get caught *in flagrante delicto* with the MD's wife.

2. Sporting Events

Another area in which you should watch your behaviour concerns intra-firm social activities, particularly sporting ones.

All winter long, the lunch hours have been dominated by idle debate about whose forehand has improved the most, or who has been sandbagging their golf handicap. Now it's early May, the weather is beginning to pick up, and the Company tennis tournament is to take place next week. What strategy should you adopt in playing that tournament ?

If you're clearly the best player in the company, the question is often decided for you : purely by chance, you'll be drawn as doubles partner of the Chairman of the Board. Play your heart out, poach shots as diplomatically as you can , apologise profusely whenever he makes a mis-

take, and make damned sure you're not knocked out first round. He didn't get where he is by being a good loser. If a red line goes through your joint names in the very first stages of the tournament, you will forever after remind him of failure and humiliation — an association that can only damage your career prospects.

Otherwise, how hard should you try ? Lots of junior executives assume that it's dangerous to beat people higher up the corporate ladder. Wouldn't it be better to flatter your superiors by letting them win ? No. Win if possible, because your opponent will know if you're better than him, and won't appreciate a public display of charity in his favour. It is perfectly acceptable to beat your superiors; just don't humiliate them. Give them what pros call a "customer's game".

If you're so bad at tennis that there's little chance of you connecting ball with raquet, let alone actually beating anyone, play with another novice on an out-of-the-way court, or put yourself in charge of refreshments. There is absolutely no correlation between sporting and business ability, but if your boss is a sporty type, it won't be beyond him to invent one. Better to go 'off-games' than demonstrate the full extent of your hand-to-eye malcoordination.

"YOURS !"

Office sporting occasions also offer a chance for colleagues to see each other in their civilian clothes — and out of them. Liberated from the strict codes of office wear, they will turn up in a delightful array of outfits, ranging from technicolour Andre Agassi to skin-tight Linford Christie.

What these costumes will have in common is a complete failure to conceal the excesses of expense-account diets — normally hidden behind loose suit jackets or dresses. Be sensitive to the feelings of your forty-two-year-old superiors who have developed paunches. Refrain from wearing miniscule French-style swimming trunks or string bikinis, even if you've been working out all winter for just this moment.

3. Management Survival Courses

The other corporate melting pot into which you might find yourself summarily tossed is the hottest and most career-threatening of all : the management survival course.

Designed to promote bonding and respect between work colleagues through a shared traumatic experience, these courses are usually run by de-sensitised ex-commandos, and involve five days of living-hell on some loveless hillside in Cumbria.

Executives whose normal idea of arduous exercise is to wheel a heavily-laden trolley around a Majestic Wine warehouse suddenly find themselves stripped naked, blinfolded, thrown into the back of a Landrover and dumped on a remote and craggy peak in sub-zero temperatures. And why ? Because the Managing Director thinks he's Gordon Burns on The Krypton Factor.

The physical and mental oppression of these courses is unremitting : So you suffer from acute vertigo ? You will climb a 70-foot flag-pole! So you're claustrophobic? Congratulations! You're in charge of the potholing expedition! To refuse means your team loses points, and in the evening everyone will sit round in an informal counselling session discussing your unco-operative, non-bonding, attitude problem. Since everyone back at the office will be dying to hear how you all got on — who was Mr Macho and who was Mr Puniverse — you can be sure that the stories will quickly become office folklore — fine if you were the hero, not so good if you were the blubbering wimp.

Whether this officially-sanctioned sadism achieves its aim of bringing colleagues together is highly doubtful. Unless you entertain fantasies about making the front cover of Soldier of Fortune, you are likely to plumb depths of misery you never knew existed, little relieved by the fact that four other tubs of lard are going through the same experience. And even if it does foster a sense of team spirit, couldn't the same effect be achieved by less primitive means — by, for instance, sending everybody off to play croquet in Cannes for a week ?

An even more appalling variation of the traditional survival course is available only to men : it is what is known as the 'Wildman' weekend, and underpinning it is the belief that since men find it harder to show their feelings, stronger-than-usual medicine is required to unbung them. The

"It's already brought us together. None of us want to go."

prescription ? A weekend camping in the New Forest, where the guys strip off, chase each other round the woods, and become abnormally open about their hidden insecurities.

The good news is that it *does* appear to work: one manager we know said that by the end of the weekend he felt like all his childhood anxieties had been lifted from his shoulders. The bad news ? Two days later, when he had to submit a report to his boss — a man who had recently been sniffing his bottom on all fours — there were lots of new anxieties to consider.

If anybody ever mentions *your* name in the context of a survival course, explain politely but firmly that you used to spend a lot of time

IN CASE OF
MANAGEMENT
SURVIVAL
COURSE —
BREAK GLASS

Lesson Nine: Doing Business in the Middle East

If you work for a large multinational company, you will, sooner or later, find yourself amidst the sands of Araby trying to bring some petro-pounds home. It's not easy. The Saudis are different from you and me. They grew up so poor that they weren't even dirt-poor : they were sand-poor. And hot. Always a new oasis, but the same damned faces.

Then one day Abdul was shootin at some food, and up from the ground came a-bubblin' crude. Black gold, Texas tea, Saudi Soda. Suddenly they were all as rich as the forty thieves.

"down at Hereford", but had to resign when you nearly killed an SAS serjeant who was stupid enough to open the flap of your tent without giving the warning signal. Add meaningfully : "I still visit the poor bugger once in a while."

If your spindly frame and concave chest make such a story implausible, at least check out what the survival course is going to involve They range from a bit of larking around on fat-wheeled Yamahas in the grounds of a country hotel to the full-blown commando bit. You don't want to roll up in your cords and Barbour expecting a gentle Blind Date weekend and find yourself in the thick of Operation Desert Storm.

Those first few billion went to buy sunglasses, air conditioners, Toyota pick-ups, more camels, and maybe a few spare wives. But with all those possessions, the Saudis started to settle down and think about business. After all, every rich Westerner they knew was 'in business'.

But what *is* business ? Simple: business is what Westerners do to make money and keep busy. But the Saudis didn't care about money. They already had more than they needed. They just wanted to get in on the fun of being businessmen : having an office, a car and a chauffeur. Getting computer print-outs. Flying Concorde to Paris for negotiations.

Drinking. Losing money at Crockfords. Keeping a mistress in Lowndes Square. And most of all, having those sweaty Englishmen in their M&S suits kiss their feet !

Thus, the cultural barriers facing a Western business executive in the Middle East are formidable. There are basically two ways of making a big impression with oil sheikhs: (1) Follow the guidelines below, or (2) Call the Prime Minister 'Mum'. History suggests that the second is the more effective ploy.

1. **Do** arrive several weeks late for your meeting. This will make your Saudi host — who is only one week late — think you are very powerful and will show your deep understanding of Arab culture. If he is upset, look at your watch and say "A thousand pardons. The traffic was heavy coming in from the airport."

2. **Do not** brush your teeth for several days before the meeting. Sit very close to your counterpart and breathe fully into his face. This is a signal in his value system that you are a person to be reckoned with.

3. **Do** season your conversation with poetic Arab phrases. Arabs have a weakness for their language, and by reciting a few well-practised lines you will show your appreciation for their culture. If you are no good at languages, at least learn enough to put forward your proposal in Arabic;

for example, *"Turiid tashtari kam ghawasaat ?"* ("Would you like to buy some nuclear submarines ?")

4. **Do not** make small talk. Saudis like to appear deep and mysterious to foreigners. They are tired of Westerners trying to break the ice with banalities like "It's not the heat that gets you. It's the humidity !" Instead, spinkle your conversation with phrases like "Oh, Mahmoud, my brother of brothers, I would joyfully travel a travel of fifty days to bring you this deal as fragrant as a thousand camels."

5. **Never** refuse coffee. The Bedouin host must serve you coffee to display his hospitality, and it is a serious insult to refuse. Even if it has the viscosity of Brent Crude, smile and drink it like a Turk. Do not ask for Red Mountain.

6. **Avoid** comments such as "Your daughter is very pretty," or "I think your wives are great !" unless you really mean it. Hospitality and generosity are central to Arab culture. When a guest speaks admiringly of a Bedouin's possessions, it creates an obligation to share them.

7. **Do not** discuss your commission in terms of 'thousands' or 'millions'. If you say "thirty-three," without adding the word *thousand*, the sheikh might write you a cheque for thirty-three *million* (all those noughts get confusing.)

THE POLICY AND PROCEDURES MANUAL

If you're one of those people who has to do everything by the book, the informal rules we've compiled in this chapter may not be enough. Find out if your company has a 'Policy and Procedures' manual, and if it does, make it your bible. The following is a sample page torn from one such corporate version of the Ten Commandments.

Sick Leave

The company allows employees five days of sick leave a year, which may be accumulated over two years. Sickness is defined as an incapacitating physical illness requiring the consultation of a doctor and necessitating at least eighteen consecutive hours of rest in bed. So-called 'mental health' days taken to extend weekends, sleep off hangovers, or do errands around the house are discouraged.

Grievences

Nobody likes a complainer, least of all your company. However, a mechanism has been created for your grievances, should you for some reason have any. Firstly, address the problem to your immediate superior. If s/he tells you where to get off, think twice about proceeding further. Approaching your boss's boss is the next step, although this is a high-risk move. If you still get no satisfaction, file a formal complaint with the required signatures of your boss and boss's boss on the appropriate form #UY-8925, available from Personnel.

Passing the Buck

The official company policy on passing the buck is not yet fully articulated. The Policy and Procedures Committee considered the issue at length before deciding to refer the matter to a firm of professional policy consultants for further deliberation.

-12-

NEGOTIATION

NEGOTIATION IS AN ANCIENT business art. It goes as far back as the Book of Exodus, when the Hebrew workers who were building the Pyramids downed tools to protest against low pay and unnacceptable working conditions. When Moses went before the Pharoah and shouted, "Let my people go," he was employing a classic negotiating technique —*making the outrageous opening demand*. When the Pharoah, in turn, refused to budge, he was simply making the standard riposte — *calling the opponent's bluff*. Finally, when Moses tired of the deadlock and asked God to visit the ten plagues upon the Egyptians, he was resorting to the oldest gambit of all — *calling in your tough guy*.

Of course, few ordinary business confrontations are of biblical importance. They just feel that way.

But the need to negotiate is a perennial part of business life, and it is worth getting a hang of the basic strategies for improving your deal.

Negotiating Thrusts and Parries

1. Drawing the BottomLine

Take the time before negotiations begin to decide what points you *must* win in order to even consider accepting a deal. If you think about these things *before* you start negotiating, you will have an anchor to support you when the sway of proposal and counter-proposal starts to unsteady your judgement.

Supposing you've never made more than £25,000 a year in your whole career, and you find yourself sitting across the table from a prospective boss who offers you £40,000 a year — and then sweetens the pot by dangling a £5000 cash bonus in front of your nose if you accept immediately. You must fight your Pavlovian response — to salivate and make an immediate grab for the cheque — and remember the £48,000 bottom line you decided on dispassionately the night before. Look your opponent inn the eye, smile confidently, and say, "I'm flattered — but I turned down two offers in the sixties earlier this week."

2. Sizing up your Opponent

Once you've decided what it is *you* want, put yourself in your opponent's shoes so that you can understand what it is *she* wants. Negotiation success isn't just about the balance of commercial power; it's also about the balance of *psychological* power. If you can get a handle on your opponent's motivations and personal weaknesses, you can steer the negotiations in the direction you want.

There are a number of ways to do this : review past correspondence, previous deals, and notes of meetings, for a start. That's obvious. But go the extra mile : have her hand-writing analysed for signs of unusual personality traits. Ask around the office to see if anyone's dealt with her before. Find out as much as you can about her business track record. All these things will help you build up a psychological profile so that you know whether you're dealing with granite or blancmange.

Staking out your opponent's home, bugging her telephone line, and rummaging through her dustbins are optional extras.

3. The Jekyll-and-Hyde Technique

Most negotiations contain elements of both competition and collaboration. That's why it's a good idea to always take at least *two* negotiators to the table. Get together with your partner the night before and decide which of you feels more comfortable playing the Hard Nut, and which of you would like to play the Nice Guy.

This ploy is particularly effective in long drawn-out negotiations where the Nice Guy can smooth things out and keep communications open, while the Hard Nut repeatedly sneers at the other side's "best offers" by walking away from the table, muttering that "Dick Turpin at least wore a mask", and declaring what a waste of time it is

*"Ignore Roy. He's just here in case we run into
any unforeseen difficulties."*

carrying on. Think of the way Nigel Mansell behaved in his wrangling with the Williams team last year. It takes an expert to make an offer of £8 million a year look like an insult.

When the Hard Nut switches to offense, he should present his inflated demands with an air of self-righteouness and inflexibility. The other side will explode with expresssions of outrage, which the Nice Guy can field with such tact and reasonableness, it will look as if he has actually switched sides.

What happens next is that the Nice Guys from both sides get together in a separate conference room for an informal discussion. They arrive at a compromise which they believe can be 'sold' to their respective Hard Nuts. On cue, the Hard Nuts suddenly moderate their demands and fade into the background while the Nice Guys sign the deal. This technique enables the Nice Guys to maximise their working relationship, while ensuring that both sides feel they have obtained the best possible deal.

---

4. Pretending to leave the "Boss" at home

A variant of the Jekyll-and-Hude technique is to leave the Hard Nut — real or imagined — at home deliberately. After reaching the outlines of an acceptable deal, you retreat from the negotiating room to a nearby office and place a call to "obtain the boss's approval". The key to this move is in leaving the door ajar so that your opponents can overhear your unsuccessful attempt to 'sell the boss'. After a few minutes of pleading, whimpering, and begging, you return sheepishly to the table with tales of how you will be hung, drawn and quartered unless you get several major concessions by midnight.

You can see this technique at work the whole time when union negotiators agree to submit a deal they have provisionally agreed with management to their members for "ratification". Surprise, surprise, the members reject the deal out of hand, and the union negotiators come back to the table with a completely new set of non-negotiable demands — supposedly insisted upon by the rank and file. In merchandising terms this technique is known as the "Bait and Switch". In negotiating theory it is known as having "multiple slices of the salami".

Note : if you don't have a boss as such, because you run your own show, you can still use this technique by casting your lawyer in the role of intractable deal-breaker, as in "I'm happy with the deal as it is, but my lawyer would kill me."

5. The Strategic Misrepresentation

It is not the place of a serious textbook to advocate the unrestricted use of wholesale porkies, but there is no harm in drawing a distinction between the "strategic misrepresentation" and the "dishonest lie".

What is a strategic misrepresentation ? Simply put, it is the equivalent of a bluff in poker : if done with finesse and in the spirit of good sportsmanship, it's all within the rules of the game.

The chief negotiator for the local government union, NALGO, might, for instance, declare that "my members are the best motivated and most efficient workers in the world". That's a harmless misrepresentation. He might continue by insisting that his rank and file would never accept anything less than a 40 per cent across-the-board pay increase. That's another harmless misrepresentation. He knows it's rubbish. His opponent knows it's rubbish. The only question is whether they will accept a 4% increase or hold out for 5%.

The dishonest lie is quite another thing, and its perpetrator must accept the possibility that his next move may be to a villa on the Costa del Sol, or a time-share rented out by Her Majesty the Queen.

Examples of the dishonest lie would include falsification of accounting documents, forgery, selling property you don't own, and using 'Sun-In'. This is not acceptable behaviour, though you should be aware of these sorts of low-pitched balls lest an over-zealous opponent try to bean you with one.

6. Choosing Sites

In most comeptitve sports, it is considered a definite advantage to play at home. This is generally true in competitive negotiation as well. As host, you have control of the agenda, the seating arrangements, and a myriad of other small factors that can put psychological pressure on the other side. If you like, you can increase the deadline pressure by insisting on taking your opponent on a two-hour tour of your office and factory, refusing to get down to business until a few hours before his train is due to leave.

Occasionally, however, you may want to do your bargaining on a neutral site, and you may even want to meet at your opponent's offices if you have something to hide — like the fact that your office furniture was repossessed last week.

7. Other Hints

• When in doubt, always say "no". It's a lot easier to reverse an initial "no" than an initial "yes".

• Go into negotiations well-rested and well-fed. Avoid drinking too much coffee so that if things drag on, you at least have a chance of winning the Battle of the Bladder.

• Avoid polarising phrases like *rip-off* or *obscene profit* (unless you are playing the role of Hard Nut)

• Include in your initial demands plenty of worthless points so that you can appear to be making generous concessions without giving anything substantive away.

• If your eyes give you away when the going gets tough, wear sunglasses.

"Well if you won't do champagne, what about wine ?"

STRATEGIC MISREPRESENTATIONS : HOW TO SUCCEED IN BUSINESS WITHOUT REALLY LYING

There are times in business negotiations when it is inconvenient — even suicidal — to tell the truth. But no ethical businessman would ever actually *lie*. Here is a list of some of the strategic misrepresentations you might come across (and use).

1. "The customer is always right."

2. It's not the lousy hundred grand that matters, it's the principle of the thing."

3. "This special sixteen-piece cruet set is not available in any store."

4. "I'm from corporate headquarters and I'm here to help."

5. "This company is run in the interests of its shareholders."

6. "The figures tell the story."

7. "To be quite honest . . . ."

8. "That's my absolutely rock-bottom offer."

CAREER
MANAGEMENT

TACTICAL
CAREER PLAYS

IN THE WORLD OF SPORT IT IS possible for players to have an enormous impact on the game at a very young age. Think of Tracy Austin, who won the US womens' singles championship aged sixteen, Gary Kasparov who became world chess champion at twenty-two, or Ian Hendry who was practically prepubescent when he won the world snooker title.

Rookie years in the business world are a little different. They may ask you to limber up before coming to the office every morning; they may put you through some arduous tackling practice and even allow you to bring on the oranges at half-time. But don't count on carrying the ball in a real game for a long time.

During the early years you might as well accept your status as a second string. There's only one way to make the team : keep your head down, listen hard during practice sessions, and do whatever it takes to catch the coach's eye when the ball comes your way. When he does finally tap you on the back and tells you you're in the team, you better have a game plan and a repertoire of moves for every possible situation. On the following pages, some of the most popular and successful career management tactics are considered.

TACTIC 1 : THE DRIVING CHARGE

This low-risk strategy requires you to hold on to the ball tightly and run as hard as you can straight at the opposition. If you adopt this tactic at the beginning of your career, you will make slow but steady progress. You're unlikely to score a try but, more importantly, you're unlikely to make some calamitous mistake which will consign you to the touch-line for the rest of your career.

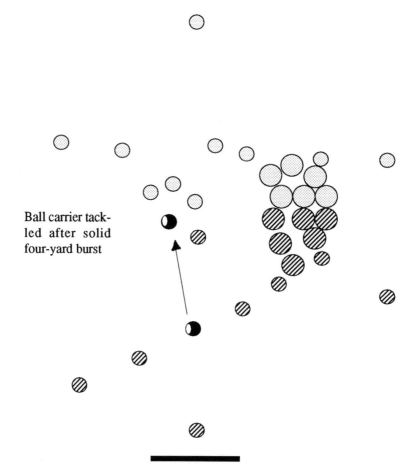

Ball carrier tack-
led after solid
four-yard burst

TACTIC 2 : THE LATERAL RUN FOR OPEN SPACE

You've been stuck in the same no-glory position for the past five years, and you can't seem to find any way through the opposition's defence. It's obvious that with your current qualifications your career path has hit a dead-end. To advance forward, you have to make a lateral move — get am MBA, an LLB or FCCA. Only then do you stand a chance of recovering some of your lost momentum.

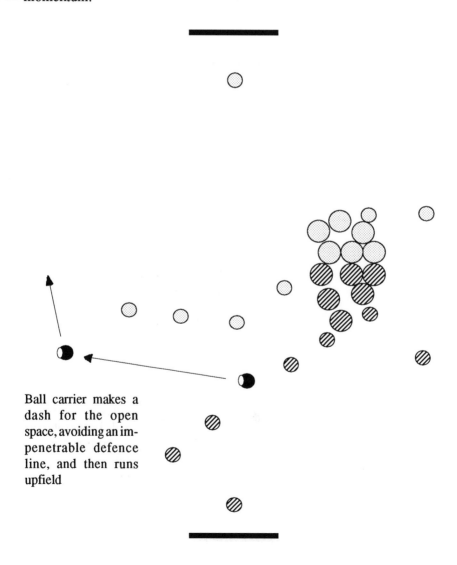

Ball carrier makes a dash for the open space, avoiding an impenetrable defence line, and then runs upfield

TACTIC 3 : THE LONG BOMB

The Long Bomb is for those who would rather be a spectacular failure than a dismal success. No longer satisfied with making four or five yards before being chopped down by the opposition, you start on a zig-zag run from your own line, aiming for the big score.

The long bomb is not for everybody, however. For evey high-scoring centre who makes the cover of the FT, there are hundreds who drop the ball in front of everybody.

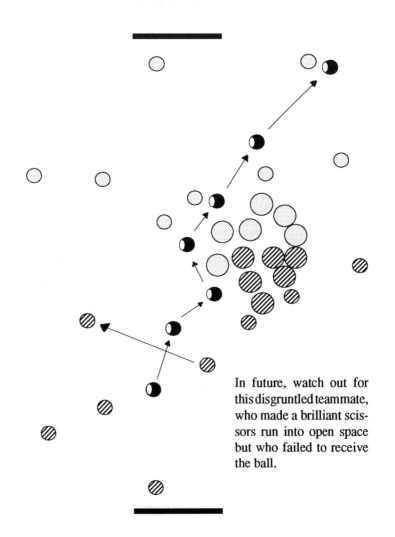

In future, watch out for this disgruntled teammate, who made a brilliant scissors run into open space but who failed to receive the ball.

TACTIC 4 : THE TURNCOAT

Tired of fighting with an uncreative coach and not having your achieve-ments recognised, you decide on a radical move. To everyone's surprise, and the opposition's delight, you hang on to the ball and run with it . . . . in the wrong direction !

The Turncoat is particularly common in the City, where dealers con-stantly switch jerseys looking for the big score. Sometimes the move is thwarted by a blitzing tackle from the team's full-back — a position often taken by the company's legal department which has previously got the centre to agree in writing that he would not switch teams.

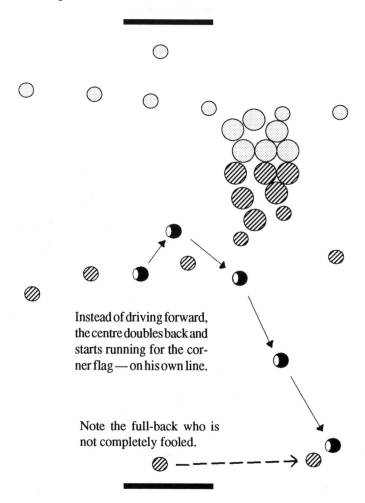

Instead of driving forward, the centre doubles back and starts running for the cor-ner flag — on his own line.

Note the full-back who is not completely fooled.

TACTIC 5 : THE PUNT

You're in over your head in a new job, or your division's had an appalling year and is losing ground rapidly. In these situations, discretion is often the better part of valour. It's time to get rid of the ball, put it in the air, and dash for safety before it lands. Top executives who resort to this tactic usually arrange a transfer to another team in advance so that they can exit quietly before the flop hits the fan. The punt is also popular with entrepreneurs who see that their hot-stock companies are about to go belly-up. They sell out to a gullible conglomerate and retire to Marbella with the proceeds.

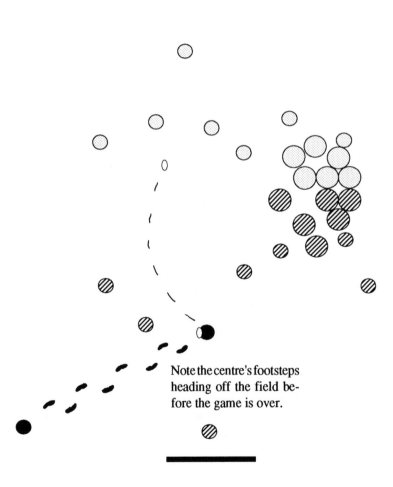

Note the centre's footsteps heading off the field before the game is over.

TACTIC 6 : THE SACK

The nightmare scenario. Your own team, tired of your prima donna behaviour, your glory-hogging runs to nowhere, and your overall cussedness on the field, decide to take you out of the game before you do any more damage to morale. To avoid the sack, be nice to your colleagues on the way up the ladder : you never know who you'll meet on the way down. And never promise more than you can deliver.

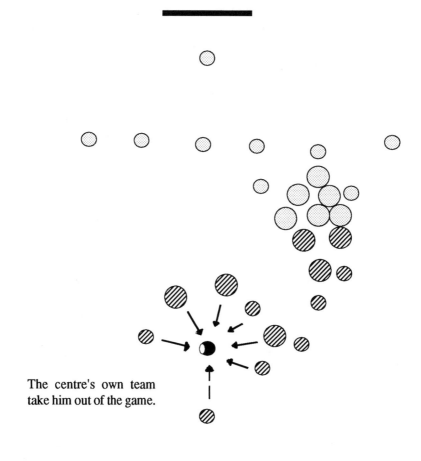

The centre's own team take him out of the game.

BEING STALKED BY A HEADHUNTER

After expanding your CV beyond recognition and interviewing for scores of jobs, you finally pick a company and start work. Your natural inclination at this point will be to roll up your sleeves and set about the task, and the last thing you should be thinking about in your first 18 months is a career move, right ?

Wrong. In the first place, many people find there is such a huge discrepancy between what they were told their job would be, and what it is actually like, that they start scanning the appointments pages within days of their arrival. In the second place, high-fliers should always stay alert to their long-term career prospects, and always be prepared to move on for the right offer.

In your first few years it is very important to catch the right wave when it comes along and, for good candidates, there will be plenty of opportunities : all the companies that rejected you a year ago for the Catch-22 of lacking experience will consider you a prime candidate for any vacancies they have in the future — now that someone else has picked up the cost of your training and your expensive first mistakes.

And now that you have graduated to the executive "after-market" you don't even have to do the legwork. Employers will approach you through headhunters.

Headhunting is a tricky business. Potential candidates have to be approached in a way which doesn't tip off their current employer, because no employer likes to think that one of their executives has got itchy feet. Consequently, headhunters usually identify themselves with a false name and firm to get past your secretary. Once *you* are on the line, they will reveal their true identity and pop the big question : for a few thousand more and a bigger company car, are you willing to walk ?

Usually the headhunter knows enough about you to bait the hook expertly. Don't ask how, but somehow she has been given your name, phone number and an old CV. You become intrigued by the glowing description of the proffered job opportunity. You set up a series of mail drops and agree on places to deposit microdots of your new CV.

Then begins a serie of clandestine telephone calls between you and the headhunter. Each time she calls your office she will give a different name and company so as not to arouse your secretary's suspicion. Most headhunters use a series of historical names so that they can remember what message they left with whom, when. e.g. the Prime Minister series : Fi *Wilson*, Sandra *Heath*, Susan *Callaghan*, Pippa *Thatcher* etc . . .

When you are the target of this flattering attention, it can be hard to keep your feet on the ground. But try to maintain a sense of reality. Remember that these corporate body-snatchers work for a client company, not for you, and that in an effort to fill a job, they are wont to dress it up in a few frills. Every position from office janitor upwards will be hailed as "exciting", "high-visibility" and "a unique opportunity". They will always be "dynamic" and the career prospects within the company will always be marvellous. You should take these and other similar claims with more salt than you'll find in a Cerebos warehouse. Remember how you expanded your CV ?

FUNCTION OF AN EXECUTIVE

As nearly everyone knows, an executive has practically nothing to do except to decide what is to be done; to tell someone to do it; to listen to reasons why it should not be done, why it should be done by someone else, or why it should be done in a different way; to follow up to see if the thing has been done; to discover that it has not; to enquire why; to listen to feeble excuses from the person who should have done it; to follow it up again to see if the thing has been done, only to discover that it has now been done, but incorrectly; to point out how it should have been done; to conclude that until it can be re-done, it may as well be left how it is; to wonder if it is not time to get rid of a person who cannot do *anything* right; to reflect that he has a wife and children, and that any successor would probably be just as bad — and maybe worse; to consider how much simpler and better the thing would have been done if one had done it oneself in the first place; to reflect sadly that one could have done it right in twenty minutes, and, as things turned out, one has had to spend two days to find out why it has taken three weeks for someone else to do it wrong.

TIME MANAGEMENT

TIME IS MONEY — AND, IF there's one thing a high-flier can't afford to waste, it's money. That's why there are numerous business books offering advice on how to manage your time. Most are two or three hundred pages long and filled with perennial time-saving tips like 'sleep less, delegate more and avoid junctions 1-30 of the M25.'

Most of these books are themselves a complete waste of time. As any time-management book will tell you, an executive's day is far too precious to waste reading anything but summaries, concise reports, and columns of figures. Here is a brief distillation of the essentials of time-management :

Find out how much Time you Waste each Day

This is easily done. Lawyers and accountants do it virtually *in utero*. Just keep an accurate diary of exactly what you have done each minute of the day. Your record should look something like the one overleaf.

Decide on your Life Strategy

A successful business career is a series of time trade-offs between your business and personal lives. Time devoted to one invariably means time lost to the other, and it's up to you to decide which gets priority.

Just drawing up a wish list is no use at all : making a few million, learning to play the ukelele, keeping fit, raising a happy family, — you might achieve two or even three of these in one lifetime, but there's no way you can bag the lot. Something's got to give.

Deciding what your priorities are requires you to formulate what is

FRUITS OF THE EARTH
COSMETICS COMPANY LTD

NAME (S. Wright)   DEPT. (Marketing)

Activity	Time Spent
Getting coffee	28 min.
Reading newspaper (horoscope, used car and help wanted ads.)	42 min.
Flirting with secretary	25 min.
Brainstorming Tomato Shampoo idea with R & D	63 min.
Completing time-sheets for personnel	21 min.
Verifying pay and working conditions of Sicilian tomato labourers	1 hr., 18 min.
Lunch	1 hr., 52 min.
Tabulating department's winnings on office Grand National sweepstake	33 min.
Talking with spouse about weekend plans	16 min.
Consideration of complete Tomato range (deoderant stick, shower gel, cream rinse and lip balm)	84 min.
Telling jokes to warehouse	10 min.
Listening to jokes from warehouse	11 min.
TOTAL	8 hrs. 43 min.

Signed ....   Date 12 / 4 / 93

known as a *life strategy*. Supposing your daughter Kylie's birthday is coming up next week — the very week you're meant to be in Jakarta to meet a key customer. You might decide to postpone that meeting on the grounds that Kylie would miss you terribly, and the first birthday's a big one. Conversely, you might take the view that it's more important to close the deal before your competitors wake up than it is to attend the party. What the hell, they don't know the difference at that age, and you can always watch the video when you get back.

No-one's saying it's easy. The temptation is to dither, and make no clear choices at all. For that reason, lots of time-management authors advocate what they call the "Armageddon Approach", which is designed to help you develop a priority list. This involves writing down your top twenty life objectives on a piece of paper and asking yourself which you would choose to accomplish if you could only complete five before the end of the world. The flaw in this approach is its short-termism : many people come out with two months in the Maldives at the top of their list.

Instead, we suggest the far more reliable 'Posterity' approach. Imagine you are writing your own obituary, and ask yourself what achievements you would like to be able to include. When you have your list of achievements, go out and realise them. Note : try to be sensible about what you include. You may have some fanciful ambition to be the first bunjee-jumper from Nelson's Column, but if you act on it, someone else may be writing your obituary sooner than you think.

Time-Management Tactics

Armed with your new life strategy, you can now move to the tactical level of time-maximisation in your business life. Start with the obvious techniques of making your memos short, dictating everything, and avoiding any meetings which aren't absolutely necessary. Refuse point-blank to sit in on administrative committees — the sort that take three months to decide whether to go with the baby-blue or buffalo-brown cups in the Maxpax machine. As anyone who has experienced them knows, committees are things where minutes are taken and hours are lost.

Get in the habit of listing all the tasks you have to achieve at the beginning of each day. Label them "Urgent", "Important but not Urgent" and "Manana". **Urgent** items might include "Attend Serious Fraud Office investigation 11 a.m." or "Catch flight to Rio 10.45 am.". **Important but not urgent** items would be "Attend Christmas Party task force meeting" or "Order new brass nameplate for office door". **Manana** is reserved for items like "Read trade magazines (*European Plastics Review, Poultry World)*" and "Get shirts laundered".

An even better way of allocating your time is to estimate how much per hour you are worth, and then select those activities which maximise your economic gain. By disciplining yourself in this way, you will avoid doing silly things like trudging all the way up Tottenham Court Road in your lunch hour to save a silly 75p on a Clayderman CD. (*Caveat* : if you are a humble shop assistant or a partner in a firm of Estate Agents, this may actually be an efficient use of your time.)

As you move up the corporate hierarchy, your implicit billing rate will rise. Adjacent is a plan of the improvements in lifestyle that should acompany each increase in your personal billing rate.

What to do when there's nothing to do

If stress counsellors are to be believed, corporate life is conducted at a furious pace nowadays, with few concessions being made to stragglers or malingerers. Executives are having to run faster and faster just to keep up, and those who are misguided enough to suffer heart attacks or nervous breakdowns are consigned to the w.p.b. for good. So the story goes. This fashionable theory ignores the fact that at some companise the executives are about as energetic as a litter of three-hour old kittens snuggled up in an airing cupboard.

Even in the most dynamic organisations, there will be odd days, weeks, even months, when there's not much to do. Perhaps you're in between projects, you're waiting for approval from above, or the courier bringing that vital document has taken a wobble speeding down the M6.

At first, these open spaces seem like a Godsend. You have time to read the paper, make a few social calls and stretch your muscles. Life seems bearable. Lady Luck is on your side.

But if you work in an open-plan office, or one of those fish-bowl ones where all the individual offices have glass walls, the enforced idleness can become excrutiating after a short time. Busyness in business is critical : *looking* as if you're hard at it when you're not is one of the most oft-neglected aspects of time-management.

Whether you find yourself in

POSITION	BILLING (£)	LIFE-STYLE
Post Room Clerk	Minimum Wage	• Take bus to work. • Cut out 10p-off coupons from office magazines before distributing them. • Lunch on sandwiches. • Take washing home to mum. • Stand on terraces at football matches.
Sales Trainee	£6.00 per hour + commission (.001 of sales)	• Commute in P-reg Triumph Spitfire • Ignore special offers except on cases of Best Bitter. • Eat in company cafeteria. • Do washing in Laundromat. • Season ticket holder at football club.
Junior Executive	£15.00 per hour	• Drive company-owned Rover 214si. • Shop for bargains on high-value goods like hi-fi, TVs, & fridges. • Eat lunch at local Italian restaurant. • Hire weekly cleaner to do washing. • Watch European football on dish.
Senior Executive	£80 per hour	• Regular plane travel, Club Class. • Price not an issue. • Eat in executive dining room. • Take on full-time housekeeper. • Sit in company box on big match days.
Managing Director	£200 per hour	• Fly first-class or in corporate jet. • Spend at least 50% of your time with your tax adviser minimising IHT. • Lunch on sandwiches; your time is too valuable to waste on formal meals. • Hire a secretary for your secretary • Buy local football club and sit in on pre-match huddle.

this predicament only once in a while, or you're holding down a job that you know is totally expendable, read, memorise and inwardly digest the following techniques of looking gainfully employed when there's sod all to do.

1. It's risky to read newspapers in open view, but if you must, have your calculator nearby, a pad of paper in front of you, and your index finger poised for a quick flip to the business section. That way, if you hear heavy footsteps while you're checking out the latest from Baz Bambigoye, it will look as if you're performing complicated multiple regression analysis. (Note : this face-saving technique will not work if you're reading the Sport, Mirror, Sun or Guardian.)

2. If you're lounging about doing nothing, and the boss's shadow looms in the doorway, grab the telephone, dial the Talking Clock, and launch straight into your customer sales spiel. Sound authoritative and purposeful, and don't rush to finish the conversation. Let your boss wait; let him think this call is important. If he's still standing around after twenty-five minutes, finish with something crisp and positive like "Thanks, Bill, I appreciate your business." or "That's the right decision, Patti. I promise you won't regret it." For added effect, leap from your chair, smack your fist into your palm, and shout "Yes! I got it ! I finally got it !" grinning all the time like the supersalesperson you are.

3. Hide in a lavatory cubicle and finish the latest Terry Pratchett.

4. Go to the stationery cupboard and search compulsively for the right coloured felt-tip.

5. Re-organise your files.

6. Insert crumpled paper into the photocopier in-tray, and push the start button. Then spend half-an-hour trying to unjam it. Repeat this procedure until (a) 5.23 pm. or (b) a smell of burning rubber and acrid black smoke starts to fill the room.

7. Rush backwards and forwards between the water-cooler, the cafeteria, the photocopier, the library and your work area, carrying an armful of computer print-outs. If anyone has the temerity to ask what you're doing, increase your pace and shout "Later, Brian, later . . . "

Apply these seven suggestions religiously, and your reputation for unfailing industry will soon earn you a private office. Before long everyone, even your superiors, will have to make an appointment to see you. By then, behind the security perimeter of an outer office, a closed door, and a loyal secretary, you're invulnerable.

WOMEN IN BUSINESS

WOMEN HAVE ALWAYS BEEN in positions of power in British buinsess. For decades, secretaries have been managing their bosses, covering up for their mistakes and taking executive decisions in their absence. The difference nowadays, is that they are more likely to achieve a rank and salary commensurate with the responsibity.

It's by no means a level playing field for women in business, but it *is* improving : most formal barriers to entry have been abolished, and hardcore chauvinists are either dying out or have learned to keep their mouths shut. This means that, as a female executive, you won't often have to put up with lecherous wolf whistles or cat calls when you walk into a boardroom. Only in a few, ultra-primitive, working environments is that sort of behaviour still regarded as acceptable. Smithfield Meat Market, Raymond's Revuebar, and Westminster Palace are obvious examples. In most companies, the spirit is more enlightened. Men recognise that they have to work with, and under, women, and most are more than happy to do so.

Nevertheless, there are still some old codgers around nurturing a fear of female competition: 'traditional ' attitudes tend to linger, like dog-muck that gets into the crevices of your tennis shoes and won't come out no matter how many times you rub them on the grass or scrub them with the washing-up brush, and you end up having to leave them outside so they don't pong up the house.

"I don't know whether you've discovered the gym yet,
but if you ever want to chat about a problem, I'm there most evenings."

Faced with such attitudes, you can adopt one of three basic positions :

The Crusader

A sort of scorched-earth approach, this involves addressing every single offence or inequity, without regard to size or context. If a male colleague offers to buy you lunch, carry your suitcase, or take your coat, you unleash a blistering barrage of feminist invective. If he asks you to get him a coffee, it's open season.

The main problem with this approach is that it requires so much energy. It's a noble battle, but exhausting.

The Mata Hari

A few women, motivated by frustration or contempt (or both), undertake to exploit those feminine resources that male executives seem most willing to recognise and reward. You can spot a Mata Hari by her black mesh stockings and garter belt.

The Survivor

Most male executives who cut their professional teeth thirty years ago occasionally need to be given a refresher course in the main tenets of sexual equality. Their hearts are in the right place; it's just that they sometimes leave their brains behind.

The Survivor Approach is a temperate way of reprogramming these fossils. It requires equal parts diplomacy, competence, thick skin and sense of humour.

> "Certainly, I'll get you a coffee Mr Hart — if you'll pick up some condoms for me when you go to lunch."

It involves not letting your core values feel threatened when you are required to endure a conversation about, for instance, whether Jimmy White should have gone for the blue in the side pocket, or played safe with the long green.

Who knows — you may even like croquet.

Whichever approach you adopt, take comfort in two things. Even the most bigoted male executive finds it difficult to sustain the myth of male superiority when confronted with the evident failure of the British economy since the last War.

Secondly, the trend is overwhelmingly in womens' favour : they are advancing steadily through the ranks of every profession and trade, (proving in the process that they can be every bit as dull and compulsive as men), and it is only a matter of time before they take their share of controlling power.

Office Romances

The traditional taboo on office romances— "don't get your meat the same place you get your bread" — should be regarded as canon law by all female high-fliers.

The risks, particularly if your chosen partner is a senior executive, are simply too great to contemplate : if you *get* preferential treatment because of the alliance, you will make enemies of everyone else in your office who will have a thousand opportunities to sabotage your career later on. If you *don't* get preferential treatment, your colleagues will still put any success you enjoy down to that two-week fling you had fifteen years ago. You can't win.

As far as *horizontal* integration is concerned (i.e. getting friendly with someone at your own level in the corporate hierarchy), the risks are fewer. People won't suspect your motives, because the alliance can't enhance your competitive position. But there's still a problem when you split up. Unless your company is huge, you're bound to bump into each other on a regular basis, and you'll still have to suffer in silence when he turns up at the Christmas party with a new companion. (Groin kicks are considered unprofessional outside Glasgow.)

The best policy is to apply a rebuttable presumption against dating your colleagues ie. it is presumed that the costs of having an affair will always outweigh the benefits, but the presumption may be rebutted in special cases. For women, such special cases are known as the "Patrick Swayze Exception"; for men, the "Victoria Principal Principle". In these cases, the costs *cannot* outweigh the benefits.

Keeping the Wolf from the Door

To make it clear that you're not available, display a photograph of your husband, boyfriend or significant other(s) prominently on your desk and drop occasional references to the fact that you played golf all weekend with "Roger". When eating alone on a business trip, bring your briefcase to the table,and pretend to go through papers from time to time. Wear a wedding ring or locket, if you've got one. All these actions will broadcast a clear message to would-be suitors, and stop you being hassled by sleazeball opportunists.

However, they probably won't be enough to deter the really assisduous Don Juans of your office from making a pass at you. Every company has at least one lecherous male executive whose only apparent raison d'etre is to bed every biped on the payroll — usually, though not necessarily, limited to the opposite sex.

This lecher may or may not be single. He may or may not be attractive. He is, invariably, smooth and confident. He will sit down in your office, cross his legs, and straighten his tie, in a slick way that says here, at last, is a guy who really knows how to sit down, cross his legs, and straighten his tie.

What you should realise, if you find yourself attracted by this act, is that you won't be sharing it; you'll be adorning it. Another notch on his bedpost.

He may come on subtly : "Amazing ! Your eyes are the same blue as my Ferrari." Or he may be more direct : "How about lunch on Sunday ? Come round early . . . . say, Saturday night." However it starts, it won't last. Afterwards, you'll just be another source of office smirks.

Making it clear that you're not interested can be difficult — and dangerous to your career, if you're dealing with the MD. Try hinting at your reservations by, for instance, telling him that your Friday nights are all booked up — for the next six years. If that doesn't work, casually mention that the office secretarial pool gave him only a '4'.

Assertiveness Training

J. Paul Getty said "The meek shall inherit the earth, but not the mineral rights."

Being sweet and agreeable is a laudable quality, but not one which is going to help you attain high-flier status. Why ? Because in every department of every company there is a certain amount of grunt work which everyone is trying to pass on to everyone else. No-one wants to do it. It gets shuffled around until, eventually, some poor succour caves in and agrees to make it his or her responsibility.

There is absolutely nothing to be gained from doing this work. No glory attaches to it if you do an excellent job — only retribution if you make a mistake. And if *you* give the impression that you're willing to eat whatever slop is put in front of you, pretty soon some of it will come your way. It will take up more of your time than you ever imagined, and leave you no chance to make an impression with other more important projects.

Lots of men would rather ask a woman to handle their grunt work than a male colleague. Typically, they'll approach it with a preliminary question like "Are you busy ?" If you answer "Not very", you'll immediately get landed with his unwanted work, and it's bound to be a nasty job or he wouldn't have phrased the enquiry in such an oblique way. If the enquiry is an even more oblique "How are you fixed for time ?" you can be sure the job has four legs and barks. The only sensible answer is an unhesitating "Very busy". Anything else, and your career will quickly turn into a remake of *'Bambi meets Godzilla'*.

On the adjacent page is an eight-week Assertiveness Training Programme. Follow the exercises carefully, and you will find after a while that fighting your own corner comes naturally.

AN EIGHT-WEEK ASSERTIVENESS TRAINING PROGRAMME

WEEK	EXERCISE
1.	Pose, hands on hips, in front of the mirror for fifteen minutes every night, repeating "No" forcefully.
2.	Buy a copy of Gloria Gaynor's "I will Survive" and memorise the lyrics. Practise singing it first thing every morning with three of four other women from the office.
3.	Dispute the bill when you next have your car serviced.
4.	Pit your driving skills against those of a London taxi driver. (If you get around town on a bicycle, leave this exercise until at least week 7.)
5.	Buy one share in British Airways, and interrupt the Chairman during the Annual General Meeting with a barbed question about business ethics.
6.	Dine at Chez Nico's and at the end of your meal suggest that the flavour of the Blanquette de Veau would be much improved by a dash of Daddy's Sauce.
7.	Take a table in the smoking section of your local pizza restaurant, and demand that the six foot-three piece of beef next to you put out his cigarette.
8.	Dial 192 and demand unlisted phone numbers.

KEEPING
SCORE

WHO'S AHEAD ?

ONE OF THE PROBLEMS OF competing in the business rat race is that it can be difficult to tell how well you are doing. The field is crowded, the start is staggered, the route is badly marked, and there's no formal awards ceremony. Sometimes it's not obvious whether you're ahead of the pack, or languishing with the back-markers.

At the beginning of your career, there is really only one indicium worth watching, though it travels under many different names : bread, dosh, dough , scratch, spondulinks, mint sauce — some have even been heard to call it "money". Those four figures on your pay slip at the end of the month may not be everything, but they are miles ahead of whatever comes second, and if you fall behind in salary, you'd be well advised to start buffing up your CV.

As your career develops, you will find that factors other than hard cash enter the 'success' equation. You will begin to covet your big office, first-class air travel, and six days a year in the company ski chalet. You will wonder how you ever coped without your chauffeur and two secretaries. You will derive more satisfaction from the increased power which each promotion brings than from the salary rise that goes with it.

When this happens don't torture yourself with the thought that you've lost your self-defining and preternatural love of money. Such feelings are perfectly natural in a highflier on the way to the top. They correspond exactly to the slightly altered version of Maslow's Hierarchy of Needs which we feature overleaf.

EXECUTIVE HIERARCHY OF NEEDS

Self-actualisation
- A secretary *still* willing to make coffee
- Appearance on the cover of The Economist
- A chauffeur
- A corner office with two windows

Self-Respect
- A reserved parking space
- An office with a door
- A pretentious title
- Share options

Survival
- A company car
- A secretary willing to make coffee
- Private health coverage
- 25 days holiday
- A job . . . any job

⬆ Begin here

Study the chart from the bottom upwards, and take note of the three levels of executive need : (a) Things needed to **survive** (b) Things needed to achieve **self-respect**. (c) Things needed for **self-actualisation.**

On the adjacent page is a questionnaire to help you evaluate your own achievements and gauge your true business status. If you finish with 400 points or more, you've already made it, and should seriously consider retiring from the eviscerating world of business in favour of a more calming life — say, painting the natives of Fiji in romantic waterfall settings.

If you score 200 to 399, book yourself in for a full cardiological examination *immediately*. You're almost at the peak, but the sheer ecstasy of getting there can be extremely hazardous, and most doctors recommend twenty milligrams of valium every six hours.

If you score less than 200 . . . well, you're never going to be the next Richard Branson, but what do you care ? Your friends like you because you're good with children and you feed stray cats. People of the opposite sex like you because you can part your hair with your tongue. What more do you want ?

If you're disqualified on more than three questions, buy a set of Stabilo highlighters, re-read this book very carefully making appropriate notes in the margin, then take the test again.

KEEPING SCORE : A CAREER EVALUATION QUIZ

Location and Type of Employment

Work at local sales office	3
Work at regional Headquarters	6
Work at Corporate Headquarters	11
Work for yourself	
At office	21
At home	5
Out of your car	Automatic disqualification

Physical Layout of your Work Area

Office with door	2
Corner Office with window	8
View of car park or air shaft	-3
View of park, river or skyline	13
Office with private bath	27
Office shared with more than two others	Automatic disqualification

Your Office Furnishings

Wall-to-wall carpeting	3
Oriental rug on polished wooden floor	9
Linoleum	-3
Chesterfield sofa & mahogany table	43
Coat hook and chair that flushes	Automatic disqualification

Telecommunications

Basic office phone	1
System incorporating E-mail, conference calls, message service etc . . .	6
As above + private line	13
Payphone only	Automatic disqualification

Secretaries & Assistants

One secretary	2
Two secretaries	4
Three or more secretaries	8
Model who can't type as secretary (if male executive)	21
Male secretary, Chippendale build, (if female executive)	35
Recent MBA asa executive assistant	16
Personal bodyguards	54
Use of secretarial pool	Automatic disqualification

Highest Business Honour or Award

Asked to join local Rotary Club	2
Elected Chairman of national trade association	12
Given honorary degree by University that kicked you out thirty years ago.	25
Biographical details in Who's Who	67
Biographical details listed in *Cyclopaedia of Super-Achievers*, Volume XLI for payment of £230 (photo extra)	Automatic disqualification

Your Personal Transport

Vauxhall, Ford or Rover	6
Jaguar, Mercedes or Lexus	12
Bentley with phone, mini-bar, Kevlar bullet-proofing and chauffeur trained in counter-terrorist driving techniques	81
Any mode of transport requiring exact change	Automatic disqualification

Business Travel

Economy Class	5
First Class	11
Concorde	35
Corporate jet + helicopter	93
Private railway carriage	117
Railway carriage shared with assorted quadrupeds	Automatic disqualification

Home Entertainment

Colour TV	2
No TV (on principle)	41
Cable/Satellite TV	6
Nintendo or SEGA system	Automatic disqualification

Home Recreational Facilities

Exercise bike or weights	3
Nautilus mahine	17
Swimming pool or Tennis court	26
Snooker table in garage	5
Snooker table in snooker room	28
Magic Finger vibrating bed	Automatic disqualification

Salary : Amount

Making your age (i.e. £25,000 for 25 year-old)	10
Making your height (in inches)	34
Making your weight (in lbs)	76
Making your shoe size	Automatic disqualification

Biggest Media Appearance

Profile in trade magazine	7
Named The Economist's 'Businessman of the Year'	46
Photographed with John Major	14
Photographed with Nick Faldo	29
Write-up in company newsletter for giving blood	-16
Grilled by John Stapleton on 'Watchdog'	Automatic disqualification

Your Personal Investments

£10,000 in high-interest Building Society account	8
Gold in Swiss bank vault	56
Equity in godson's business	-12
A collection of Cigarette cards	Automatic disqualification

Tax Affairs

PAYE only	5
Schedule D with envelope of receipts	-2
Administered from Grand Cayman	67
Pay more to tax lawyers and accountants than you would have to Inland Revenue	Automatic disqualification

"I'm done with sex, and Lord knows I've made enough money, but power — that's something you never get tired of."

BUZZWORD GLOSSARY

In *'My Fair Lady'* Professor Higgins manages to pass off an ordinary flower girl as an elegant member of London society by teaching her a few polite phrases. Similarly, the high-flying executive, by careful study over several gruelling years, can blend effortlessly into boardroom life by mastering a key collection of buzzwords.

Spend a few weeks memorising all of the following terms and shorthand abbreviations. Then practise them with friends so that you can slip them naturally into your conversation. When you achieve a rate of eleven B.P.M. (buzzwords per minute), you will be ready to talk your way into a high-visibility job at just about any company you want.

AA The second-highest rating issued by the Standard & Poor's rating service. Also refers to an organisation which re-treads bottle-fatigued executives.

Battle of the Bladder
An extremely risky negotiating technique in which adversaries ply each other with innumerable cups of coffee over an extended period, and see who has the greater will-power and endurance.

Beta
A measure of the systematic risk inherent in a portfolio of stocks. Often used to describe risk as a generic concept, as in "Nicky, you're a tiger, but I need more stability in my life. Your beta is a little too high."

Business Ethics
1. The code of conduct to which high-flying executives should subscribe. 2. An oxymoron ranking up there with "abstract art".

Cannibalisation
The phenomenon by which increased sales of a new product are achieved by cutting the heart out of the sales of an old product. (see missionary selling)

Cash Flow
1. The amount of cash earned by a business, calculated by adding depreciation and deferred taxes to reported earnings. 2. A term used by executives to describe their personal financial predicament, as in "Could you lend me a couple of hundred for the weekend ? Just tide me over till the cash flow improves."

Corporate Vietnam
A devastating phrase used to put down another executive's pet proposal, as in "Go head-to-head with Grecian 2000 in the male hair-colouring market ? What are you trying to do, Jim, get us into some kind of Corporate Vietnam ?"

C.Y.A.
'Cover your Arse'. The overriding principle behind most executive decisions. If you ignore it, and things go wrong, you may find yourself being invited to "an interview *without coffee*".

D & B
Dun & Bradstreet. A service that performs credit checks on other companies.

Driven
Another A.P.B. (all-purpose buzzword) used as a suffix to describe what makes a particular business or industry tick; thus "production-driven", "marketing-driven", "technology-driven" and so on. Also used to describe the character of certain executives.

Dynamic
An A.P.B. adjective used by headhunters to describe any unfilled job or any burned-out executive they are trying to place. Also used as a noun by securities salesmen in lieu of words their customers might actually understand, as in "It is our opinion that the distributed software dynamic is *the single most important* trend in technology . . . Paradyne's products all participate, one way or another, in this major technology dynamic."

E.D.P.
'Electronic Data Processing'. For non-computer-minded executives, synonymous with IBM, Unisys, Digital etc . ..

E.P.S.
'Earning per share'. The primitive yardstick used by most shareholders to evaluate a company's performance. Also often used by non-ex-

ecutive remuneration committees to determine the Managing Director's annual bonus. Consequently, many top managers devote more time to managing E.P.S. than they do to managing the company.

FIFO/LIFO

"First in, last out" and "Last in, first out". Two different methods of accounting for inventory and the cost of goods which a company sells. FIFO assumes that the oldest goods in inventory are sold first; LIFO assumes that they are sold last. During periods of high inflation, the choice of FIFO or LIFO can have an enormous effect on profitability, because new inventory will always cost more than old inventory. A crowded carriage on the Underground uses LIFO principle, whereas a crowded restaurant uses FIFO.

Goodwill

A company's intangible assets, like its brand name, reputation, or dealer network, which are thought to be crucial to its earning power. e.g. the name 'Selfridges' enjoys considerable goodwill, 'Ratners' less so.

Hidden Agenda

A person's *secret* motivations. For example, if a civil servant negotiating a juicy government contract is quibbling over insignificant terms in the contract, his or her secret agenda

might be to stall until you agree to reconvene negotiations in a more congenial spot like Paris or the Seychelles.

I.R.R.

'Internal Rate of Return'. The implied rate of return on an investment, assuming complete reinvestment of cash flows.

Learning Curve

A theoretical curve describing the reduction in production cost achieved by a company as it gains experience in making a product. Now adapted for popular use, as in "When I first started reading the FT, it took me three hours to plough through it. Now I can skim it in ten minutes, so I suppose I'm coming down the learning curve."

Leverage

1. A measure of the amount of money a company or person borrows relative to its net worth. Thus, a company with £50 million in net worth, and £100 million in borrowings, is using two-to-one leverage. 2. A term used by executives in non-financial contexts, as in "How I'd manage without my two assistants I don't know. They really leverage my time."

Liquidation

Generally, the disposal of assets through sale or abandonment. In certain "family-controlled" industries, however, it refers to the disposal of competing management personnel. (see Corporate Strategy *ante*)

Management
The art of getting other people to do the dirty work. (Warning: after Hercules cleaned out the stables, he put Augeus to the sword for giving him such a dreadful job.)

Maturity
1. The date on which bonds or loans become due and payable. 2. The stage in a product's life cycle when growth in sales has slowed (see Marketing *ante*) 3. A quality of character, the lack of which is often displayed by executives haggling over the location of their car-parking spaces.

M.B.A.
Acronym for several different but related terms : 1. Master of Business Administration 2. Master Bullshit Artist 3. Master of Blind Ambition.

Missionary Selling
Preaching the value of certain products or services to the non-believing buyer. (see *Cannibalisation*)

Mushroom Theory
Refers to the way most corporate research and development is done. The theory states that if you put a

bunch of boffins in a dark room and dump a pile of manure on them, something useful might come up.

Mutual Fund
A vehicle for investing in diverse stockmarket portfolios which are professionally mis-managed.

N.P.V.
'Net Present Value'. The value of projected cash flows returned by an investment, *discounted* back to the present. For example, the N.P.V. of the £300 per week you expect to get from your private pension in twenty years' time, discounted back to the present at averaged inflation rates, will be worth about enough to buy you a Pot Noodle.

Number-Crunching
Spending late nights working out numbers on a spreadsheet. Recently recognised as the cause of one of bsuiness's most debilitating diseases, the formation of painful calluses on an executive's two index fingers which are detrimental to his or her golf swing.

Opportunity Cost
The implicit cost of missing an opportunity because you or your capital were busy elsewhere. e.g. the two years of salary missed while you did an M.B.A.

Overheads

The fixed, unavoidable costs of operating a business. Examples include the cost of manufacturing facilities for an industrial company, the Chairman's Daimler, the corporate jet, and the company suite in the Savoy. The money to pay for these and other essentials is raised by levying overhead contributions on the profitable operating divisions of the company.

Par

1. The stated guaranteed liquidation value of one ordinary share in a company, often £1. 2. An *acceptable* performance, as in "The division's peformance was up to par." 3. In golf, a score of one stroke per hole more than your client.

Parent Company

A holding company that owns a controlling interest in another company. The trend of rapid acquisitions and de-mergers over the last ten years make many of these so-called 'parent' companies look more like foster parents than natural ones.

Psychological Contract

The *unwritten* understanding between employer and employee, as in "Asking me to pick up your dry cleaning is not only **not** in my job description, it's a gross violation of my psychological contract !"

Reactive/Proactive

A *reactive* executive responds to problems after they happen, whereas a *proactive* one anticipates them. Executives who use this phrase inevitably characterise themselves as proactive.

Recession/Depression

Recession is when your neighbour loses his job; depression is when you lose yours. These economic downturns are notoriously difficult to forecast, but sophisticated econometric modelling houses like that of the CBI have correctly predicted fourteen of the last three recessions.

Risk/Return

The generally positive relationship between the returns of an investment and the risk involved in making it. Translation : "No guts, no glory."

R.O.I.

"Return on Investment". In French, the word roi means king. In the short-term world of British business, the acronym R.O.I. *is* king. It is the driving force behind most strategic decisions, as it expresses the amount of profitable bang a company can get for each invested buck.

Sale/Leaseback

An arrangement whereby one company sells assets to another, then leases them back. Purposes : (a) to raise quick cash, and (b) to transfer tax benefits like depreciation to a company that has income to deduct them from.

Scenario
An imagined sequence of events that provides the context in which a business decision is made. Scenarios always come in sets of threes : best case, worst case, and just-in-case.

Secondary Market
An exchange or market where previously-owned assets are traded. Examples : the London Stock Exchange, the Hang Seng, the Bourse, Stringfellows.

Sensitivity
1. The degree to which an action will affect a given measure of performance, as in "Our profitability is very sensitive to market share." 2. *(archaic)* The ability of a manager to relate to the problems of his subordinates.

Short-term Optimiser
A term used to describe executives who make decisions with an eye on the next quarter's financial statements rather than the long-term health of the company. Antonym of big-picture thinker. Sometimes used as a synonym for M.B.A.

Synergy
A critical buzzword. See the 'Finance' chapter for a detailed explanation.

System
Another A.P.B., used to describe every imaginable aspect of business or the economy. Thus, financial system, accounting system, monetary system, distribution system, production system, and so on, ad infinitum. Advertising copyrighters recognise a good buzzword when they see it — hence a sachet of car shampoo and a sponge becomes "the complete car care system".

Upstream/Downstream
Describes the acquisition by a business of related manufacturing or marketing capabilities. If Kodak were to buy a chain of shops in the high street to sell its film, it would be "integrating downstream". When, earlier this century, it bought a farm to raise horses in order to process them into gelatin for film manufacture, it was "integrating *upstream*".

U.S.P.
"Unique Selling Point". *The* most important all-purpose buzzword for marketing executives. The U.S.P. for *Penthouse*, for example, is the magazine's artistic integrity. If your product doesn't have it, go back to the drawing board.

THE FORMULA FOR SUCCESS

$$\text{Success} = \left[A \left(\frac{C \times N^2}{E} \right) + P(B)^3 + G \right]^L + W$$

Key

A = Ambition
B = Buzzword proficiency
C = Curriculum Vitae expansion
E = Excessive educaton (Phd, M.B.A., etc . . .)
G = Gold handicap
L = Luck
N = Nerve
P = Power accessories
W = Work

Also Published by Harriman House

'The Official
Lawyer's Handbook'

Can you spot the lawyer ?

"One of the most irreverent, funny, and perceptive books about the legal profession ever published." The Times

"The *Spitting Image* of the legal world: irreverent, biting, and often in delightfully questionable taste." The Lawyer

" . . . . combines a litany of barbed quips with sound advice." The Law Society Gazette

"A jokey guide to the sleazy world of the solicitor, full of sage advice." The Independent on Sunday

Including advice on the following critical areas :

• Twenty good reasons to become a lawyer: Why not? Everyone else is.
• Law Society Finals: thousands of morons have passed them. So can you!
• How to get into a top law firm — and stay there.

• Crucial legal skills: (a) sucking up to secretaries (b) making clapped-out photocopiers work (and vice versa)
• Drafting legal documents: more is better . . . . until it begins to make sense.
• Weekend work: avoiding it, simulating it, surviving it.
• The creative art of billing: who says there are only 24 hours in a day ?
• The heavenly state of partnership: is something amiss in paradise ?
• How to end a legal career: explain to a client how the time he's been billed for was *really* spent.

• The lawyerly look: a wardrobe as dull as your work.
• How to handle romantic feelings towards a lawyer and what to bring with you on your first date.
• Lawyers and sex: the erotic power of Latin

ORDER FORM

NAME   _____

ADDRESS   _____

TEL.   _____

Please send me one copy of the *OLH* at £8.20 incl. P & P. I enclose a crossed cheque payable to 'Harriman House'

Philip Jenks
Harriman House Publishing
PO Box 482
London
SW6 4XL

SIGNED

_____

DATE

_____